# FAMOUS, INFAMOUS & FORGOTTEN

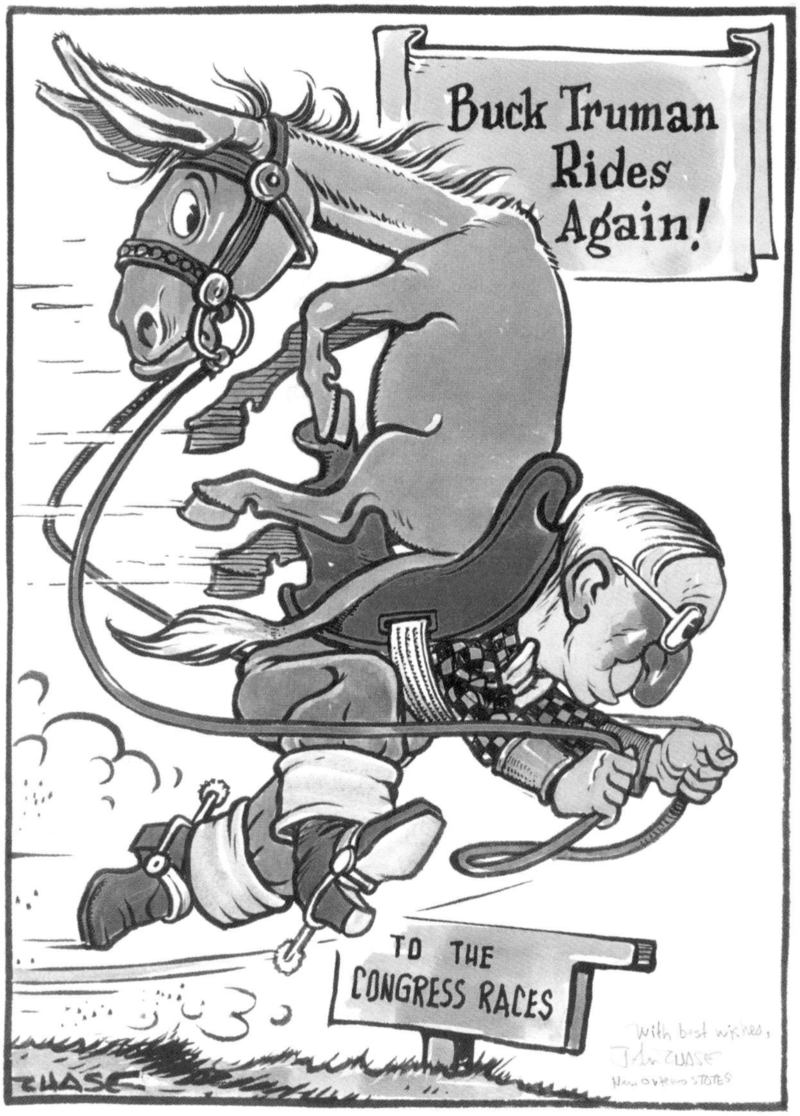
Buck Truman Rides Again!
TO THE CONGRESS RACES
CHASE
With best wishes,

576

ITEM 73 JOHN CHASE, *BUCK TRUMAN RIDES AGAIN*

# Famous, Infamous & Forgotten ❦ ❦ ❦

❦ Political Cartoons from the Collection of *Anthony J. Mourek*

❦ Exhibited from 14 November 2013 through 10 January 2014

❦ *The Grolier Club*, in the City of New York ❦ M M X I I I

This exhibit catalog is not for sale and is "strictly for nonprofit educational purposes."

ISBN: 978-1-60583-051-3

# Contents

# ❦ Introduction

<hr>

*"Better, better far, there had been no art, than thus to pervert and employ it to purposes so base and so subversive of everything interesting to society."*
James Barry (1741–1806) Irish Artist

*"Stop them damn pictures. I don't care so much what the papers write about me. My constituents can't read. But, damn it, they can see pictures."*
William Magear "Boss" Tweed (1823–1878) American Politician

I grew up in a home fascinated with politics and political cartoons. At that time, Chicago had four major daily newspapers, each with at least one locally based political cartoonist. Every day these newspapers were delivered to our home, and each day we discussed their political cartoons.

Through this process, I grew to appreciate how art could be used as a weapon to attack, to defend and to comment on political figures and issues. I have been interested in this process as an art form since first being introduced to political cartoons published in daily newspapers. But if not for a gift from my father, I may not have become a collector of original drawings.

My father was on the board of a company that decided to create a Civil War collection with the help of book dealer Ralph Newman. When he visited Newman's shop, Ralph took a John T. McCutcheon cartoon from a large stack he had in his office and gave it to my father. My father, in turn, gave it to me, and that became the first item in my political art collection.

From McCutcheon's drawing of a long-forgotten Chicago mayor, my collection has grown into thousands of original drawings of political cartoons, 18th- and 19th-century British and Irish prints, posters, books, sculptures, oil paintings, political pottery and even wood block prints of the Sino- and Russo-Japanese Wars.

Long before the word *caricature* existed, an ancient Egyptian artist took a break and drew what we would now identify as a caricature on a hidden wall. Sixteenth-century Italian artist Annibale Carracci gave us the word caricature. But the world had to wait for the combination of relatively cheap means of reproduction combined with prosperity and a developing democratic system to create a market for the first true political cartoons in 18th-century Britain.

The first political cartoons were single sheet copperplate engravings that were often beautifully hand colored. The engravings were expensive for the average British subject and often included long explanatory texts. They were principally aimed at the literate political elite in London and in the great country houses. Some could only be completely understood by those elites. But they were widely distributed and affected opinion throughout the British Empire.

Of the many early cartoonists, the most important was James Gillray. He is often called the father of the English political cartoon. Gillray was bigoted against Catholics, the Irish and foreigners. He was sometimes in the pay of special interests and died mad in a fall from his publisher's roof. Yet he created the Anglo-Saxon world's image of Napoleon, and his cartoons illustrate modern histories of his time.

The market for political cartoons expanded in 19th-century Britain and America due to a growing middle class and less expensive means of reproduction used by popular magazines like *Punch* (1841), *Harper's Weekly* (1857), *Puck* (1871) and *Judge* (1881). Many great magazines like *The Masses* (1911) continued the tradition into the 20th century, but as the magazines closed, political cartoonists transitioned to the editorial pages of the many daily print newspapers.

Most educated Americans know the names of two cartoonists—the one they saw in the newspaper this morning and Thomas Nast. Nast was America's first great political cartoonist. He created our images of Santa Claus and the GOP elephant. Nast usually is remembered for his good government anti-Boss Tweed cartoons and his strongly pro-Union Civil War cartoons for which Lincoln called him "our best recruiting sergeant." Yet, like Gillray, Nast sometimes was in the pay of special interests and drew many bigoted cartoons attacking Irish immigrants, their Church and blacks. In 1886 he left *Harper's Weekly* and his career slowly declined. He died in 1902 of yellow fever as US consul general in Guayaquil, Ecuador.

Art Young is my favorite political cartoonist even though I rarely agree with his political viewpoint. In his 60-year career (1883–1943), he moved from being a traditional Republican to being a left wing socialist who was tried for sedition. At first, Young drew Nast-like cartoons, but slowly he developed his own distinct style, which I find very appealing.

The print newspaper is now a dying institution. Each year fewer print newspapers exist, and each year those that remain employ fewer political cartoonists. From the 18th-century hand-colored engraving to the online publications of today, much has changed, but much is the same. An artist, a drawing and an idea remain, although there may not be anything on paper to collect. The future of the political cartoon may be with young artists drawing on their iPads for Internet blogs, for which they may or may not be paid.

The English-speaking world's political cartoon tradition is the oldest and the most sophisticated. Many other traditions exist, but most have been influenced by the Anglo-Saxon tradition. The history of these traditions I leave to others who are less Anglo- and American-centric.

Nearly a half-century of collecting has led me in many directions, but I always return to my first interest: original drawings of political cartoons that illustrate political figures and issues that are recognizable to me. I have long been a member of the Manuscript Society, currently serve on the board and am a past president. Why, you might ask, would a person who collects art be a member of the Manuscript Society? My answer has always been that I consider political cartoons historical documents at the intersection of politics, history and art.

Each original drawing can be viewed from many differing perspectives: as the artist intended it to be seen, as seen by the viewers of the day and as seen by the viewer today. The political cartoonist, like the writer, makes a political point. However, we can never truly understand what the artist intended or what the original viewers saw without historical knowledge. That knowledge will always be imperfect, subject to speculation and affected by our own beliefs.

My goal in this exhibit is not to present a detailed history of the political cartoon as an art form but to display a small sampling of political cartoons from my collection of thousands of items. I have organized the exhibit to give an overview of the breadth of the collection in the limited space available while choosing favorites and arbitrarily focusing on *racism, the forgotten* and *the unexpected.*

Viewing each work in its historical context, as this exhibit attempts to do, provides insights as to how artists used literature and sociocultural symbols to depict political figures and define political issues. Cartoons often used literary references, Greek mythology and even movie themes to make political points. The use of cultural stereotyping was prevalent. One cannot appreciate the artist's intent without understanding the historical perspective.

The original drawings in this exhibit allow you to see the art as only the publishers and editors of their time viewed them. Historically, readers only saw greatly reduced poorly printed images. The original art was typically drawn on poor quality paper or board for publications that often ended their days wrapping fish. Until recently, the original art was often discarded or given away. As a collector it is my mission to help in the preservation of this art form.

It was impossible to include many of my favorite items and cartoonists because of space limitations, terms of the exhibit and theme. Preference in selection was given to original drawings over prints and prints over other objects. Some items were also rejected because of poor condition or because they were even more offensive than those chosen.

# ACKNOWLEDGMENTS

The original drawings of political cartoons that survive do so only because of luck and the few individuals and institutions that found them of value. I'd to like to thank the many artists, collectors, dealers, heirs and conservators who made this collection possible.

This exhibit and catalog was made possible through the assistance of my archivist and co-author Valerie Higgins (Fermilab archivist and historian) and the project administrator Rosanne Schultz (CPM and friend). But most of all, this exhibit was made possible by my wife Dr. Karole Schafer Mourek, who encouraged me to organize my collection, and Saundra Taylor, who recommended Valerie.

In addition I wish to thank Dr. Tim Benson for his advice on catalogs and cartoons; Laura Ten Eyke for help with provenance research; Despina Kotsapouikis and Kiki Labrou for Greek translations; Teresa Marrandino and Karen Slavik for layout advice and media descriptions; Bozena Pszczulna-Szymanski for conservation; David Jones for printing the blocks better than they had ever been printed and many others who helped with the exhibit or catalog, including those at the Grolier Club like Andrew Berger, Eric Holzenberg, Jennifer Sheehan, Jerry Kelly, George Ong, Maev Brennan and Megan Smith.

# Catalogue

## I ❧ The Forgotten (and Soon-to-be Forgotten)

Since political art is devoted entirely to current events, political cartoons of the past frequently depict people, events, and viewpoints that were well-known at the time of cartoon's creation, but are now less well-known or in the process of fading from public consciousness. These cartoons serve as unique, engaging documents of their times. While people who have held such offices as vice president of the United States or Speaker of the House often play pivotal roles in the politics of their times, such people are rarely as well remembered as presidents. Even some presidents are only passingly familiar to many modern citizens. This phenomenon can also lead us to reflect on which of today's household names are likely to be all but forgotten in a hundred years.

1) FRED OPPER *Another president who had a rise in the world. "From the toepath to the White House."*

Ink drawing, 24 × 31 cm. / October 19, 1881 / Published in *Puck* (New York City)

In this cartoon, President Rutherford B. Hayes (in office from 1877 to 1881), dismisses future President Chester A. Arthur (in office from 1881 to 1885) from his post as collector of the Port of New York by kicking him out onto a road which leads to Washington, D.C. President Ulysses S. Grant appointed Arthur to the post in 1871.[1] Arthur was part of a faction of the Republican Party led by Senator Roscoe Conkling called the "Stalwarts," who relied heavily on political patronage[2] and he received his position through this system.[3] Rutherford B. Hayes, who ran on a platform of reform, was selected as the Republican presidential candidate in 1876 and won that year's election. In 1878, Hayes dismissed Arthur as part of his efforts to reduce corruption in the American political system.[4] Following James Garfield's nomination as the Republican presidential candidate at the contentious 1880 Republican convention, Arthur was nominated as his running mate in an effort to make peace with the Stalwarts, who had supported former President Grant. Garfield won the election, and when he was assassinated in July of 1881, Arthur became president of the United States,[5] just two years after he was dismissed from his position as collector of the Port of New York by Hayes.

U.S. presidents of the late 19th century are often less familiar to Americans today than those of earlier and later eras, but, as this cartoon demonstrates, there were a wealth of political dramas at the time that inspired cartoons like these. Such cartoons let us see these dramas through the eyes of the people who experienced them.

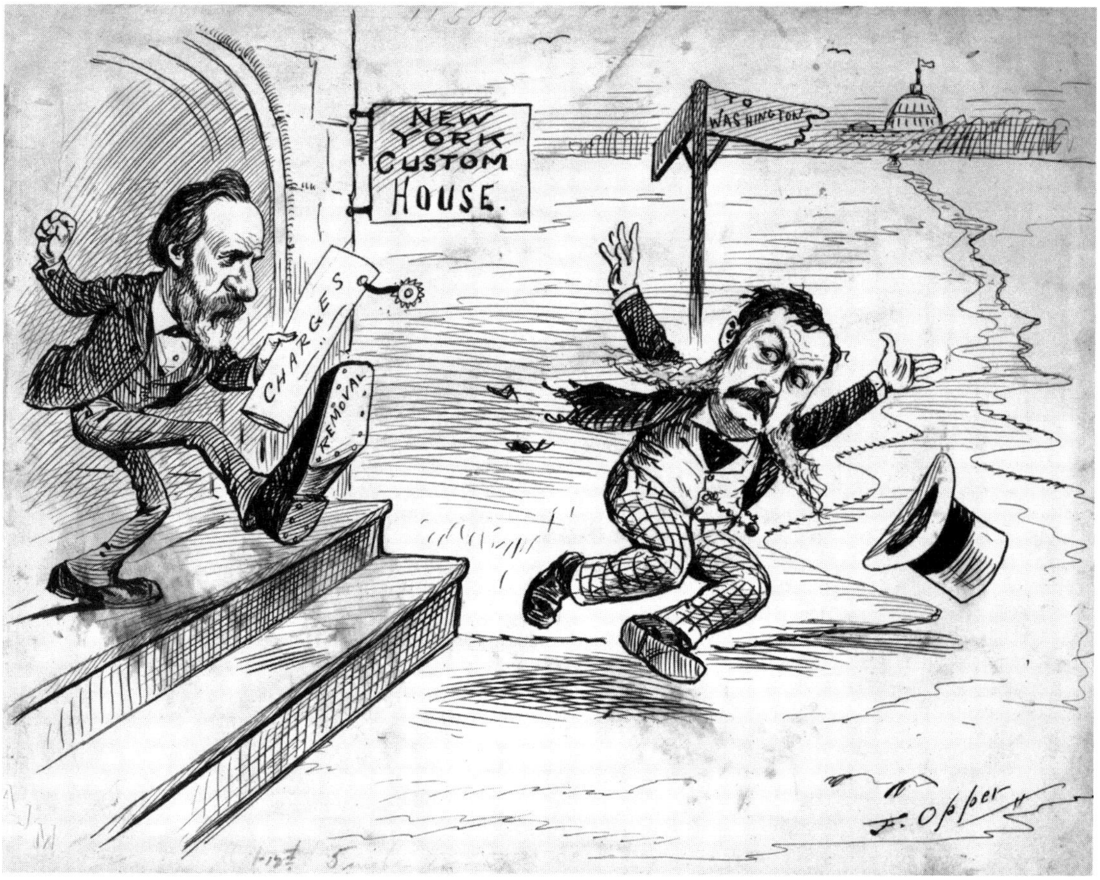
NEW YORK CUSTOM HOUSE.
TO WASHINGTON
CHARGES
REMOVAL
F. Opper

ITEM 1

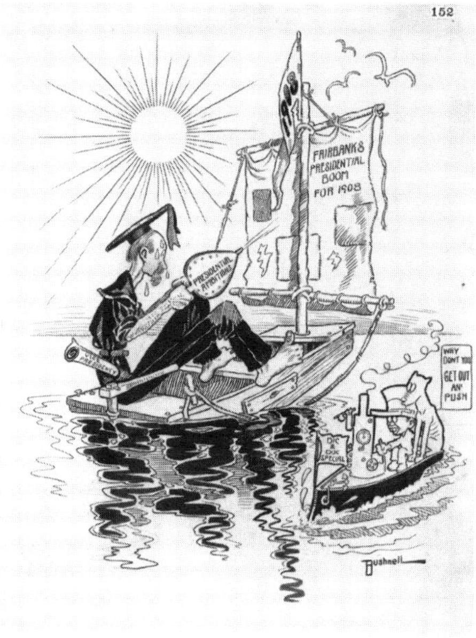
152
FAIRBANKS PRESIDENTIAL BOOM FOR 1908
WHY DON'T YOU GET OUT AN' PUSH
Bushnell

ITEM 2

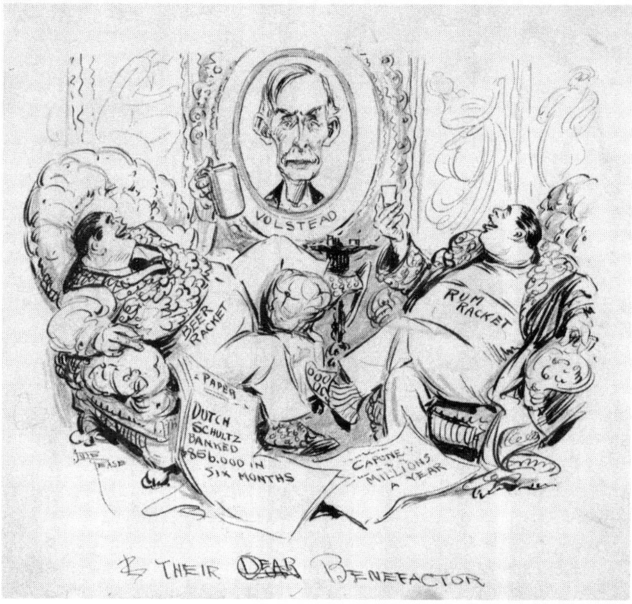
VOLSTEAD
BEER RACKET
RUM RACKET
PAPER
DUTCH SCHULTZ BANKED $86.000 IN SIX MONTHS
CAPONE MILLIONS A YEAR
THEIR DEAR BENEFACTOR

ITEM 3

## 2) ELMER A. BUSHNELL *Sailing, sailing*

Ink drawing, 45.7 × 37 cm. / 1907 / Published in the *Cincinnati Times-Star* (Cincinnati, Ohio)

In this cartoon, Charles W. Fairbanks, vice president of the United States from 1905 to 1909 under President Theodore Roosevelt, struggles to propel his boat labeled "Fairbanks Presidential Boom for 1908" with only the small, hand-held bellows of his "presidential ambitions" for power. Fairbanks sought to fulfill these ambitions during much of the first two decades of the twentieth century, but he experienced a series of near misses. Today he is probably better known as the namesake of Fairbanks, Alaska than as a man who might have been president.

In 1900, the Republican Party nominated William McKinley for reelection as president, and the leaders of the party considered nominating Fairbanks as the vice-presidential candidate. However, Fairbanks, who was a senator from Indiana at the time, chose to remain in his position, hoping to run for president after McKinley completed his second term in 1904. The Republican Party selected the charismatic Theodore Roosevelt as the 1900 vice-presidential candidate instead. When McKinley was assassinated in 1901, Roosevelt became president. He proved to be so popular that the Republican Party did not seriously consider nominating anyone else to run for president in 1904, so Fairbanks accepted the vice-presidential nomination that year, hoping to be nominated as the presidential candidate in 1908. Roosevelt, however, did not like Fairbanks, who was supported by the more conservative elements of the Republican Party. When Roosevelt chose not to run for reelection in 1908, he supported the nomination of William Howard Taft for the presidency rather than Fairbanks. This cartoon refers to the dashing of Fairbanks's presidential hopes by Roosevelt's endorsement of Taft.

Fairbanks sought the Republican presidential nomination again in 1916, but he was again unsuccessful. This time, the Republican Party nominated him as Charles Evans Hughes's vice-presidential candidate. Hughes and Fairbanks narrowly lost the election to Woodrow Wilson and Thomas Marshall.[1]

Like many American vice presidents, Fairbanks is hardly remembered today. His decisions, however, paved the way for the much more well-known Theodore Roosevelt to become president, and, had events transpired a little differently, Fairbanks might have been president. Fairbanks was just one of many vice presidents whose presidential ambitions were unfulfilled. See, for instance, items 11 and 58 depicting Hubert H. Humphrey.

This cartoon is also an interesting example of the occasional overlap between editorial and gag cartoons. Unlike editorial cartoons, gag cartoons simply illustrate a joke or entertain the viewer without making a political point. Bushnell drew both types of cartoons, and this cartoon includes a reference to some of his gag cartoons in the form of a man, Dic, and a dog, Doc, who comment on Fairbanks's situation. They are seated in a tiny tugboat flying a banner that reads "Dic and Doc special." Doc was a popular canine character Bushnell used in his gag cartoons,[2] and Dic is presumably the man riding with the dog.

## 3) LUTE PEASE *Their dear benefactor*

Ink drawing, 24.3 × 29 cm. / 1925 / Published in *Newark Evening News* (Newark, New Jersey)

In this cartoon, mobsters Al Capone and Dutch Schultz toast a portrait of Representative Andrew J. Volstead of Minnesota, who is identified as "their dear benefactor." The National Prohibition Act, which was introduced by Volstead and nicknamed the Volstead Act, was enacted in 1919 to implement the Eighteenth Amendment,[1] which prohibited the production, transportation, and sale of alcohol in the United States. Ironically, Prohibition led to the rise of organized crime as mobsters like Capone and Schultz stepped in to meet the American public's continuing demand for alcohol.[2]

While Prohibition-era gangsters like Al Capone and Dutch Schultz are still familiar to most Americans, the congressman behind the legislation that led to their rise is less well-known.

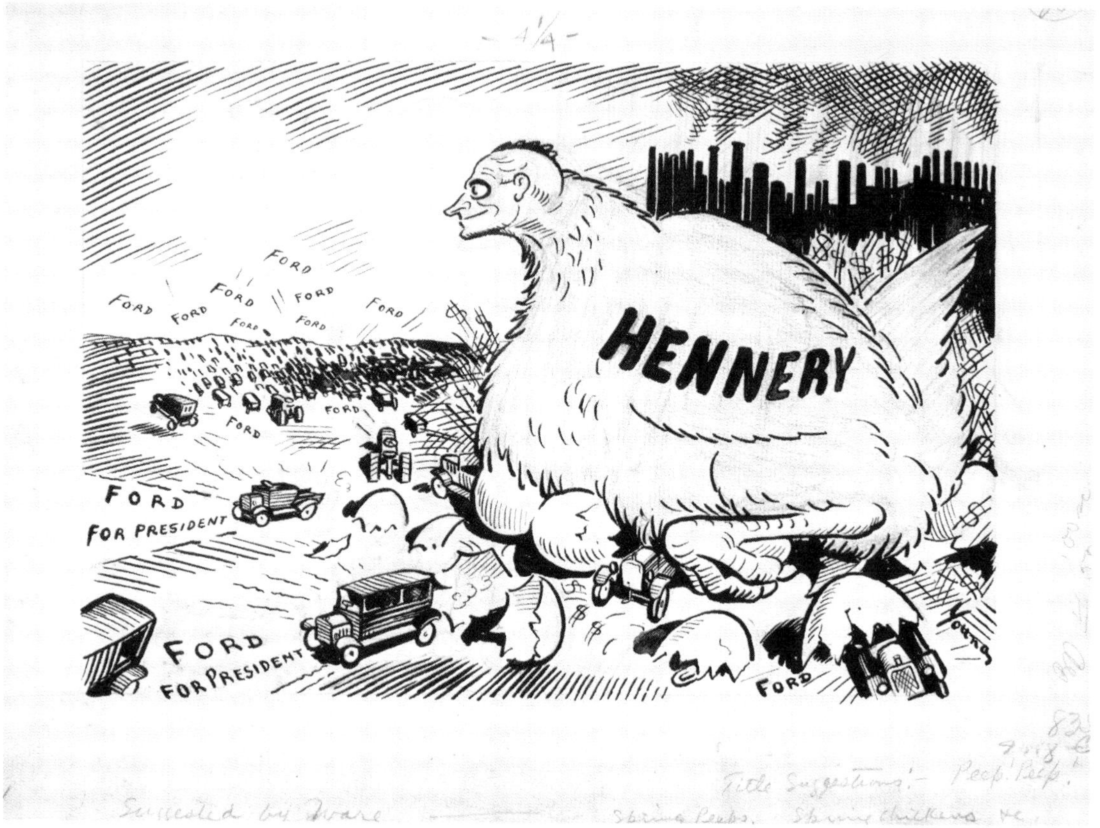
HENNERY
FORD
FOR PRESIDENT
FORD
FOR PRESIDENT
FORD

## 4) ART YOUNG *Ford for President*

Ink and colored pencil drawing, 19 × 29.5 cm. / c. 1916–1923 / Published by Life Publishing Company

While Henry Ford is best known for founding the Ford Motor Company, introducing the Model T automobile, and developing the assembly line,[1] this cartoon refers to the industrialist's less well-known role in politics. In this image, a large hen with Ford's head sits on a clutch of eggs from which Model T automobiles are hatching, their horns tooting the slogan "Ford for President." This cartoon refers to the grassroots enthusiasm for Ford as a candidate for president which sprang up between 1916 and 1924.

At the time, many people had a positive impression of Ford, who appeared to have socially progressive views. In 1914, he offered his workers a salary of five dollars a day, more than twice what most other companies offered.[2] Ford also characterized himself as a pacifist, even sponsoring the European Peace Expedition or "peace ship" in 1915, a private diplomatic mission to Europe which Ford hoped might help bring World War I to an end.[3] All these things made many Americans see Ford as an appealing candidate for president.

In 1916, Henry Ford, without campaigning,[4] won the Michigan Republican presidential primary election with 83,038 votes.[5] Ford did not progress beyond this point in the 1916 presidential election. In 1918, he ran for the U.S. Senate as a Democrat, but was narrowly defeated.[6] After this lackluster performance, Ford made no further attempts to seek political office. While Ford did not actively seek the presidential nomination, this didn't stop "Ford-for-President" clubs from forming in Michigan and elsewhere in the United States to promote him as a candidate for the 1924 election.[7] Only when Ford endorsed President Coolidge for reelection[8] did this enthusiasm wane.

Today, it is hard to imagine Ford as a popular candidate for president, since he is often associated with anti-Semitism[9] and resistance to unionization.[10]

## 5) ART YOUNG *Vice-President Marshall walks like Charlie Chaplin*

Ink drawing, 17 × 24.5 cm. / c. 1916 / Publication status unknown

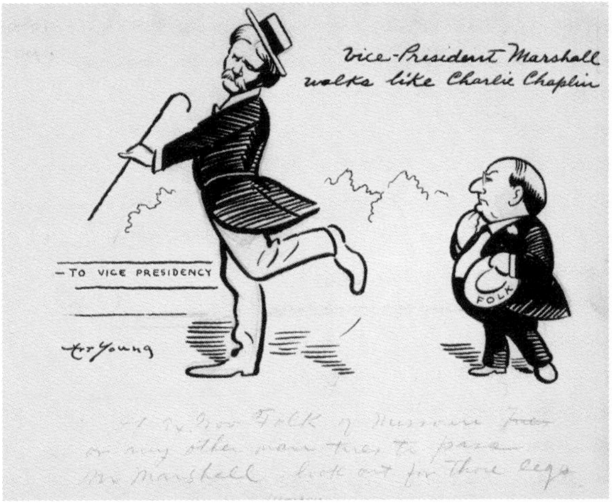
Vice-President Marshall walks like Charlie Chaplin
— TO VICE PRESIDENCY
FOLK
Art Young

*Caption:* "Vice-President Marshall walks like Charlie Chaplin. If Ex. Gov. Folk of Missouri or any other man tries to pass Mr. Marshall—look out for those legs."

In this case, the popular culture reference Young uses in the cartoon is likely to be more recognizable to modern viewers than the subject of the cartoon. Young has depicted Thomas Riley Marshall, U.S. vice president under President Woodrow Wilson from 1913 to 1921,[1] as Charlie Chaplin's famous "Little Tramp" character.[2] Joseph Wingate Folk, who was governor of Missouri from 1905 to 1909[3] and moved to Washington, D.C. in 1912 to work for the State Department and Interstate Commerce Commission,[4] looks on as Marshall imitates Chaplin's characteristic walk.

Although Marshall was known for poking fun at the office of vice president as an ineffectual one, once describing his position as being like that of "a man in a cataleptic fit; he cannot speak; he cannot move; he suffers no pain; he is perfectly conscious of all that goes on, but has no part in it,"[5] vice presidents can, in fact, play a significant role in the course of the country. Marshall, for instance, refused to take over as president when Wilson was incapacitated by a stroke,[6] and the lack of strong leadership during Wilson's illness is sometimes cited as a contributing factor to the failure of the United States to join the League of Nations.[7] In any case, Marshall is likely to be only passingly familiar to most viewers. Folk has been all but forgotten, and the exact circumstances to which this cartoon refers are difficult to determine. The reference to Charlie Chaplin, however, is still widely recognizable.

## 6) ART YOUNG *The Cabinet of Doctor Cali-Coolidge*

Ink drawing, 37 × 28.5 cm. / December 1927 / Published in *New Masses* (New York City)

This cartoon makes very effective use of a popular culture reference that modern viewers are likely to be less acquainted with than contemporary audiences. The cartoon's title refers to the 1920 German film *Das Kabinett des Dr. Caligari*, which is translated into English as *The Cabinet of Dr. Caligari*. In this film, the character Dr. Caligari runs a sideshow that features a fortune-telling somnambulist, Cesare, whom Caligari keeps in a cabinet. During the course of the film, the protagonist discovers that Caligari has been controlling Cesare and using him to commit murders by proxy.[1] The film created a strong reaction among American audiences when it was released.[2]

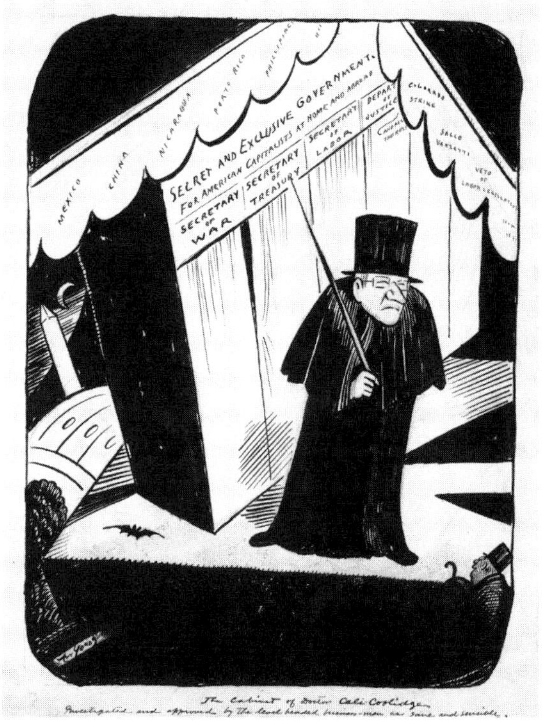
MEXICO
CHINA
NICARAGUA
PORTO RICO
PHILLIPINES
SECRET AND EXCLUSIVE GOVERNMENT.
FOR AMERICAN CAPITALISTS AT HOME AND ABROAD
SECRETARY OF WAR
SECRETARY OF TREASURY
SECRETARY OF LABOR
DEPART OF JUSTICE
COLORADO STRIKE
SACCO VANZETTI
VETO OF LABOR LEGISLATION
The Cabinet of Doctor Cali Coolidge
Investigated and approved by the level headed business-men as sane and sensible.

ITEM 6

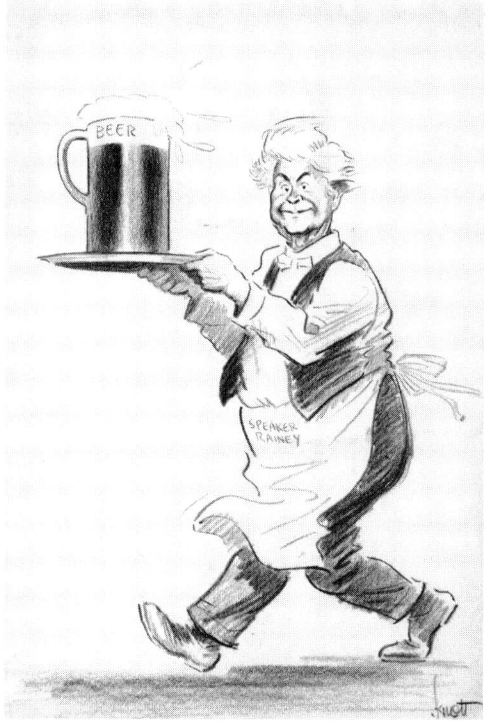
BEER
SPEAKER RAINEY

ITEM 7

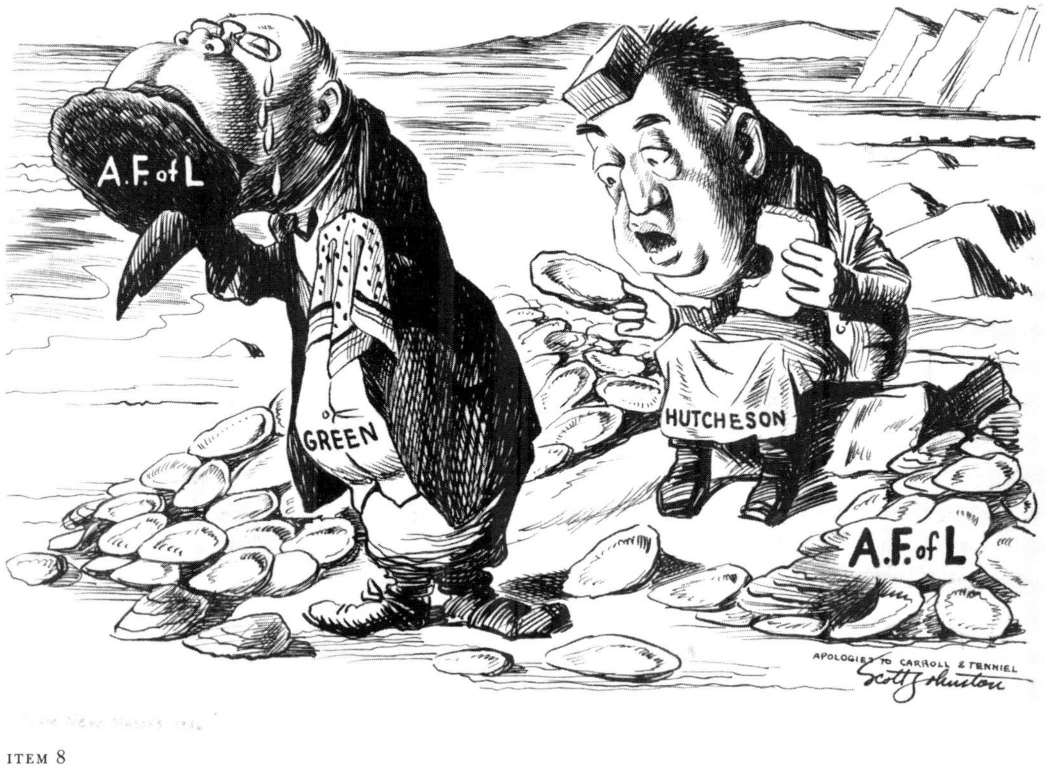
A.F. of L
GREEN
HUTCHESON
A.F. of L
APOLOGIES TO CARROLL & TENNIEL
Scott Johnston

ITEM 8

In this cartoon, Young has dressed President Coolidge as the sinister Dr. Caligari, echoed the cubist aesthetics of the film, and covered the cabinet behind him with references to aspects of Coolidge and his presidency that Young found problematic. These include Coolidge's dealings with organized labor, which were not always sympathetic;[3] the Sacco and Vanzetti case, a controversial trial in Massachusetts while Coolidge was governor of that state in which two Italian immigrants were convicted of murder and sentenced to death on largely circumstantial evidence;[4] and his foreign policy towards Latin America, which included support of strong U.S. business ties and maintenance of U.S. peacekeeping forces in some Latin American countries.[5] Young, who was a well-known socialist,[6] is likely to have viewed the conservative, business-friendly Coolidge[7] as a villainous figure.

## 7) JOHN KNOTT *What this country needs is more liquid assets*

Pencil drawing, 36 × 26.3 cm. / 1933 / Published in *Dallas News* (Dallas, Texas)

Like vice presidents, Speakers of the House of Representatives have also played key roles in the history of the United States, but are rarely well remembered. This cartoon depicts Henry Thomas Rainey, a representative from Illinois who was Speaker of the House from 1933 to 1934.[1]

While Rainey was Speaker for only a short time, this period included President Franklin Delano Roosevelt's first hundred days in office, during which Congress passed much momentous legislation aimed at alleviating the conditions of the Depression.[2] This included the passage of the Cullen-Harrison Act, which legalized the production of beer with a 3.2% alcohol content months before the official repeal of Prohibition. President Roosevelt sent a message to Congress on March 14th, 1933 requesting that they pass such a bill to raise tax revenues and provide a boost to American agriculture and manufacturing. Representative Cullen of New York introduced the bill to the House of Representatives on March 15th, and the House passed it that same day.[3] The Senate passed the bill on March 20th,[4] and President Roosevelt signed it into law on March 22nd.[5] This cartoon refers to the passage of the Cullen-Harrison Act by depicting Rainey as a waiter delivering beer to the country.

Rainey also presided over the House during the passage of the Twenty-first Amendment, which repealed Prohibition and was ratified on December 5, 1933.[6]

## 8) SCOTT JOHNSTON *The walrus and the carpenter*

Ink drawing, 24.5 × 36.5 cm. / 1938 / Published in *New Masses* (New York City)

*Caption:* "The walrus and the carpenter. 'I weep for you,' the Walrus said: 'I deeply sympathize.' With sobs and tears he sorted out those of the largest size, holding his pocket handkerchief before his streaming eye."

This cartoon depicts William Hutcheson and William Green, two influential labor leaders who had a profound impact on the American labor movement, but are not household names today. William Green was president of the American Federation of Labor (AFL) from 1924 to 1952.[1] William Hutcheson was president of the United Brotherhood of Carpenters and Joiners, which was affiliated with the AFL, from 1915 to 1952.[2] The AFL, founded in 1886, originally included only skilled craftsmen,[3] and both Green[4] and Hutcheson[5] were hostile toward the growing movement to include unskilled, industrial workers in its ranks. In 1935, the leaders of this movement formed the Committee for Industrial Organization (CIO) within the AFL, and, for a time, they sought to reform the AFL from within. However, Green and the other leaders of AFL ultimately expelled CIO from the organization in 1937. In 1938, CIO reorganized itself as the independent Congress of Industrial Organizations.[6]

In this cartoon, drawn shortly after the AFL and CIO split, Johnston takes the part of the CIO by employing a reference to a passage from Lewis Carroll's *Through the Looking Glass* and its accompanying illustration by Sir John Tenniel as an elaborate metaphor.

The caption of the cartoon is a direct quote from the poem "The Walrus and the Carpenter," which Tweedledee recites to Alice in *Through the Looking Glass.* In this poem, a walrus and a carpenter are walking along a beach when they encounter a bed of oysters. The pair invites the oysters to accompany them on their walk, and, after leading them far from their bed, they proceed to devour all the oysters. The walrus weeps with apparently false sympathy for the oysters as he sorts out and eats the best ones. Johnston based his drawing on Sir John Tenniel's illustration of this episode in Carroll's novel.[7] The walrus has William Green's face, while the carpenter, appropriately, bears the face of William Hutcheson. The stack of discarded oyster shells is labeled "A.F. of L." Johnston seems to be suggesting that Green and Hutcheson are predators, leading the members of the AFL astray and working against them, all while pretending to sympathize with their struggles.

The cultural references in this cartoon are particularly interesting, since Johnston clearly expected his audience to be familiar not only with the episode of the walrus, the carpenter, and the oysters from *Through the Looking Glass*, but also with Tenniel's illustration of the episode. Item 56 in this exhibition is an illustration of the widely known Tenniel, and item 62 is a cartoon drawn by him.

## 9) PAUL PLASCHKE *Mouthpiece*

Ink, crayon, and Ben-Day overlay* drawing, 27.3 × 25.5 cm. / May 21, 1948 / Published in *Chicago American* (Chicago, Illinois)

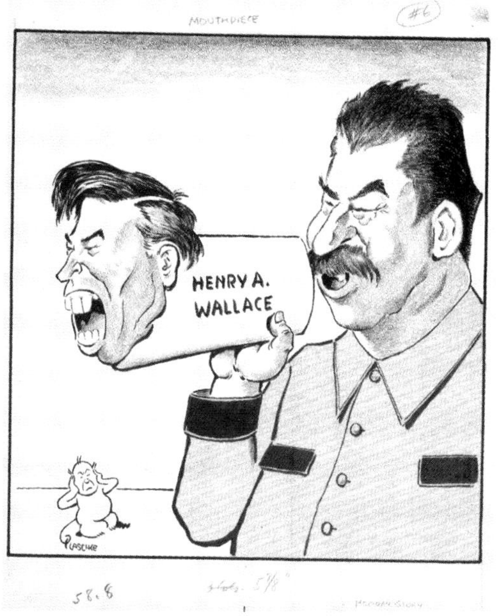
MOUTHPIECE
#6
HENRY A. WALLACE
PLASCHKE

This cartoon shows Henry A. Wallace as a mouthpiece for Soviet leader Joseph Stalin. The Democratic Party nominated the progressive Wallace as its candidate for vice president in 1940 at President Franklin D. Roosevelt's insistence, despite the resistance of many Democrats. Wallace served as vice president for one term, from 1941 to 1945. In 1944, Roosevelt gave in to pressure from the members of his party who wanted a more conservative vice-presidential nominee and accepted Harry Truman as the candidate. Had Roosevelt not compromised, Wallace would have become president at Roosevelt's death rather than Truman. Instead, Wallace became secretary of commerce after completing his term as vice president. He served in this position from 1945 to 1946, first under President Roosevelt, and later, after Roosevelt's death, under President Truman. Wallace and Truman frequently came into conflict over Truman's dealings with the Soviet Union, however, since Wallace advocated for less confrontational relations with that country. After Wallace publically criticized Truman's policies, Truman demanded his resignation.[1]

*Ben-Day overlays are transparent sheets covered in evenly-spaced dots that some cartoonists use to create shading effects in their drawings. The artist cuts the shape of the shaded area out of the sheet and attaches it to the drawing.

In 1947, Wallace announced that he would run for president as a Progressive Party candidate. His support of greater cooperation with the Soviet Union led many to dismiss him as a "communist dupe" and "Stalinoid,"[2] and this cartoon is one of those criticisms. The Communist Party of the United States endorsed Wallace's candidacy on August 2, 1948,[3] which cemented his unpopularity among most Americans. In some locations, Wallace's appearances were met with jeers and flying eggs[4,5]. Wallace did not receive any electoral votes in the 1948 election, and he never held a major political office again.[6]

Wallace is not well remembered today, but at one time he was a divisive figure in American politics, and, had Roosevelt held firm in his support of Wallace in 1944, Wallace might have been president of the United States. Had that been the case, international politics likely would have taken a very different course. Wallace, for instance, was a vigorous opponent of the Marshall Plan, the U.S. program to supply aid to foreign countries to stimulate their recovery after World War II.[7] Wallace argued that the plan would only benefit business leaders and would increase international tensions.[8] Had he been president, it likely would have never been implemented. Wallace was also critical of the North Atlantic Treaty Organization (NATO), an alliance between a dozen Western nations that was established in 1949.[9] Wallace argued that such an organization would simply antagonize the Soviet Union.[10] Had Wallace been president, it is possible NATO would not exist today.

## 10) DAVID LOW *Peaceful war news*

Ink and crayon drawing, 28 × 41.7 cm. / March 20, 1953 / Published in the *Manchester Guardian* (Manchester, England)

This cartoon was published just two weeks after Josef Stalin, the leader of the Soviet Union, died on March 5th, 1953.[1] It reflects the power vacuum left by his death and the skepticism of the Western world about the trustworthiness of the Soviet Union as a new government took over and the Cold War continued to escalate. On Stalin's death, Georgy Malenkov became main party secretary and chairman of the Council of Ministers, a position analogous to prime minister, but there were many others also vying for power.[2]

In the cartoon, Malenkov speaks while his associates and rivals sit just behind him. While we cannot be entirely certain about the identities of the seated figures, the following are our best guesses, from left to right: unknown, Anastas Mikoyan, Nikolai Bulganin, Lazar Kaganovich, Vyacheslav Molotov, Lavrenty Beria, and unknown.

While Malenkov claims that the Soviet Union loves peace, he is interrupted by a reporter announcing that the Soviet Union has shot down two friendly planes. This probably refers to two incidents that occurred shortly before the cartoon was published. In the first, two United States F-84 Thunderjets were attacked by Czechoslovakian jets on March 10th, 1953, with one shot down over West Germany, near the Czechoslovakian border. The Czechoslovakian government defended the actions of its pilots, saying that the American planes had violated their airspace.[3] In the second, two Soviet planes shot down a British bomber at the border between East Germany and West Germany on March 12th, 1953, killing five of the seven people on board. The two incidents, coming so close together and so soon after a new Soviet government had come to power, increased tensions between the Soviets and the West.[4]

This image provides a snapshot of a period of time when no one man had yet emerged as a clear successor to Stalin and the Soviet government would soon be shaken by in-fighting and power struggles.

While Malenkov was chairman of the Council of Ministers, Malenkov and Nikita Khrushchev soon entered into a power struggle. Khrushchev became first secretary of the Soviet Central Committee in

September of 1953,[5] and in 1955 he was able to demote Malenkov to a relatively minor position[6] and replace him with his close associate, Nikolai Bulganin.[7]

Beria, Molotov, Bulganin, and Kaganovich became first deputy chairmen of the Council of Ministers shortly after Stalin's death,[8] but they too would all fall from power within a few years. Khrushchev had Beria, who was an ally of Malenkov, arrested in June of 1953. Beria was tried and executed in December of 1953.[9] In 1957, Molotov, Malenkov, and Kaganovich led a group of Soviet politicians within the Politburo who attempted to oust Khrushchev from his position. Khrushchev forced the Politburo to get approval from the Central Committee, which reversed the Politburo's decision. This gave Khrushchev the opportunity to dismiss the three from their positions. Khrushchev cemented his power by removing Bulganin from his position in 1958 and taking the position himself, making Khrushchev head of both the Communist Party and the Soviet Union.[10] Mikoyan was the only member of Stalin's original Politburo to support Khrushchev in the 1957 conflict, and he played an influential role in Khrushchev's government until 1964, when he was appointed head of the Soviet government and Leonid Brezhnev replaced Khrushchev as first secretary of the party. Mikoyan retired from politics in 1975.[11]

At the time of the creation of this cartoon, it was unclear how these political maneuverings would unfold, and all these Soviet politicians are depicted on relatively equal footing. It is likely that all these men would have been recognizable to British viewers of the time.

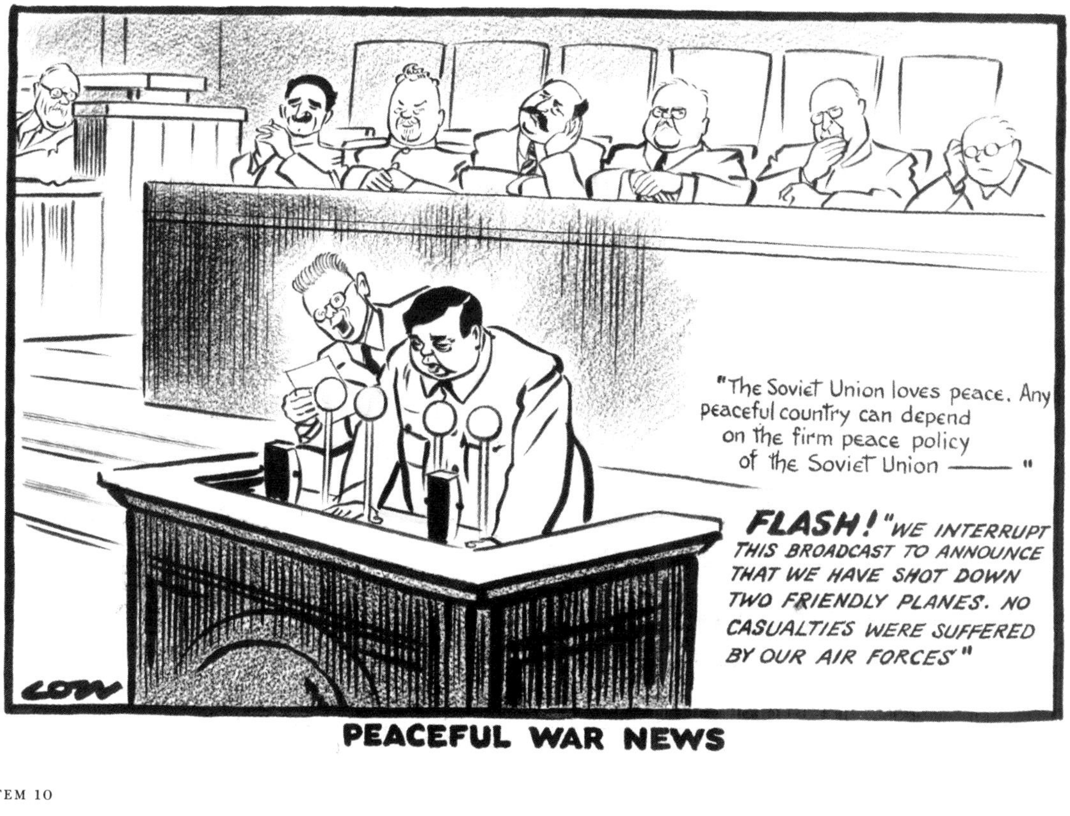
"The Soviet Union loves peace. Any peaceful country can depend on the firm peace policy of the Soviet Union —— "
FLASH! "WE INTERRUPT THIS BROADCAST TO ANNOUNCE THAT WE HAVE SHOT DOWN TWO FRIENDLY PLANES. NO CASUALTIES WERE SUFFERED BY OUR AIR FORCES"
LOW

PEACEFUL WAR NEWS

ITEM 10

## 11) JOE PARRISH *Me and my shadow*

Ink and watercolor drawing, 23.3 × 26 cm. / October 16, 1968 / Published in the *Chicago Tribune* (Chicago, Illinois)

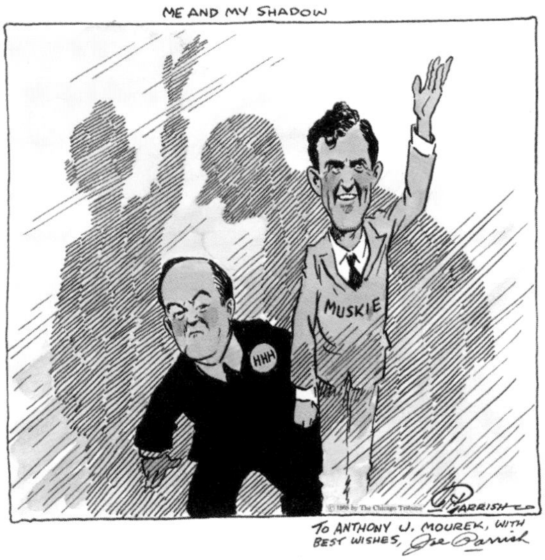
ME AND MY SHADOW
HHH
MUSKIE
PARRISH
TO ANTHONY J. MOUREK, WITH BEST WISHES, Joe Parrish

Hubert H. Humphrey served as vice president under President Lyndon B. Johnson from 1965 to 1969. Before he became vice president, Humphrey was an often outspoken proponent of liberal policies. While serving as Senate majority whip, Humphrey was instrumental in securing the passage of groundbreaking legislation, such as the Peace Corps, Medicare, the first nuclear test ban treaty, and the 1964 Civil Rights Act.

Initially, Humphrey hoped to play an influential role in the Johnson administration's policies. Johnson, however, granted his vice president little power or influence, and he responded to dissent from Humphrey by shutting him out of decision-making meetings. Humphrey soon fell into line with Johnson's policies in order to maintain favor with the president, which diminished his influence and relegated him to the role of a supporter rather than a leader. When Johnson chose not to seek reelection in 1968, the Democratic Party nominated Humphrey as its presidential candidate at the controversial 1968 Democratic National Convention in Chicago. Senator Edmund S. Muskie of Maine was his running mate.

Unfortunately for Humphrey, his attempts to remain in favor with Johnson made many Democratic voters see him simply as an extension of Johnson with no positions of his own.[1] Humphrey would later say, "After four years as Vice President... I had lost some of my personal identity and personal forcefulness... I ought not to have let a man who was going to be a former President dictate my future."[2] Muskie, on the other hand, was popular with Democratic voters, and some political commentators of the time argued that Muskie would make a better presidential candidate than either Humphrey or his opponent; Richard M. Nixon.[3] This cartoon reflects these attitudes. Humphrey is nearly hidden behind Muskie, his running mate, and Humphrey does not cast a shadow of his own; instead, he is shadowed by the shape of Johnson. The divisions within the Democratic Party weakened the Humphrey-Muskie campaign, and they ultimately lost to Nixon, the Republican candidate, by one of the smallest margins ever in an American presidential election.[4]

The exhibition history of this particular cartoon demonstrates how once well-known political figures can quickly fade from the public's memory. All the figures in the cartoon would have been recognizable at the time of its creation. When it was exhibited at the Union League Club in 1987, they were still familiar to most viewers. Today, however, Humphrey and Muskie are likely to be recognizable to far fewer people. This cartoon also demonstrates how the place of political cartoons in the public discourse has changed over time. When this cartoon was published, it was printed in color on the front page of the *Chicago Tribune*. It is unlikely that an editorial cartoon would receive such prominent placement today.

## 12) CHRIS RIDDELL *Monica under spotlights*

Ink and watercolor drawing, 24.5 × 32 cm. / 1998 / Published in the *New Statesman* (London, England)

On December 19, 1998, President Bill Clinton was impeached by the U.S. House of Representatives on charges of perjury and obstruction of justice. The charges were prompted by Clinton's attempts to conceal the affair he had with young White House intern Monica Lewinsky from 1996 to 1997.

During Clinton's 1992 campaign, his opponents accused him of acting illegally in his dealings with a company called Whitewater Development Corporation. After Congressional hearings on the issue, Clinton agreed on January 12, 1994 to appoint an independent counsel to investigate. The first counsel, appointed by Attorney General Janet Reno, found no evidence of wrongdoing. He, however, was replaced in July of 1994 by Kenneth Starr, who was appointed by a three-judge panel under the Independent Counsel Reauthorization Act.

In a separate scandal that was initially unrelated to Starr's Whitewater investigations, Paula Jones filed a sexual harassment lawsuit against Clinton on May 6, 1994. Jones's lawyers began investigating Clinton's past, hoping to find evidence of other incidents of sexual harassment to strengthen their case. They learned of Lewinsky's affair with Clinton, and they eventually passed this information along to Starr, who was still looking for evidence of any wrongdoing by Clinton. On January 12, 1998, Starr received concrete evidence of the affair from Lewinsky's acquaintance Linda Tripp. On January 17, Clinton testified in the Paula Jones case, using evasive language that some would later consider perjury to conceal his affair with Lewinsky. Ultimately, Clinton's affair with Lewinsky became public knowledge through Starr's investigations, and on August 17, Clinton admitted in a nationally televised press conference that he had misled the American people about the nature of his relationship with Lewinsky. He maintained, however, that his testimony in the Jones case had been legally accurate. Starr submitted a report to Congress on September 9 in which he charged Clinton with numerous impeachable offenses. On December 19, the House of Representatives voted to impeach Clinton on charges of perjury and obstruction of justice. After the Senate trial that followed the House impeachment vote, the Senate voted on February 12, 1999 to acquit Clinton of the charges. Nonetheless, the proceedings surrounding the Paula Jones case and the impeachment had turned into a media circus, and the press published many lurid details of the affair between Clinton and Lewinsky.[1,2,3,4,5] Today, the details of Clinton's affair with Lewinsky are more widely remembered than the details of his alleged perjury.

This cartoon depicts the scandal from a British perspective, and it is more a comment on the reaction of the American public to the scandal than the scandal itself. Lewinsky is depicted as a ridiculous but harmless-looking figure, while two much more sinister figures, one dressed as a puritan and the other as an unsavory-looking reporter, leer at her. The artist Chris Riddell seems to be characterizing the fascination of the American public and news media with the affair as both puritanically disapproving and tawdrily voyeuristic. Additionally, Riddell has depicted Monica herself as a huge figure that fills the spotlights, which seems to be a comment on the fact that it was Clinton's affair rather than his perjury that took center-stage in the American media and the court of public opinion. Ironically, while Riddell's reporter and puritan are very American figures, the British media and public have not been immune to being distracted from the pertinent facts of a political scandal by tangential sexual elements. In 1963, British Secretary of State for War John Profumo had to resign from his position after he lied in the House of Commons about his affair with a young woman named Christine Keeler. The public and media, however, focused less on the issue of Profumo's lies and more on the rumors that Keeler had also had an affair with Eugene Ivanov, the naval attaché at the Soviet embassy. While Clinton successfully weathered his impeachment and the media scrutiny Riddell criticizes, Profumo's career was ruined.[6]

Despite his impeachment trial, Clinton has remained an active figure in Democratic politics since the end of his second term. In time, it is likely that the impeachment trial and the intense scrutiny of Clinton's affair with Lewinsky will be little more than a historical footnote.

## 13) PAUL THOMAS *P. G. Wodehouse was a traitor*

Ink and watercolor drawing, 17.3 × 24.5 cm. / September 17, 1999 / Published in *The Daily Express* (London, England)

P. G. Wodehouse is best remembered as a humorist and the creator of the characters Bertie Wooster and his trusted valet, Jeeves.[1] This cartoon references a lesser-known episode in the author's life during World War II.

Wodehouse and his wife were living in Le Touquet, France when it was occupied by the Nazis, and he and other foreigners were interned by the German Army in July of 1940. Shortly after his release in June of 1941, the German Foreign Press Office asked Wodehouse to do several broadcasts to America, so Wodehouse wrote and performed a series of broadcasts titled "How to Be an Internee in Your Spare Time Without Previous Experience" that were humorous reflections on his life during his internment. The broadcasts outraged members of the British government and press, some of whom accused Wodehouse of writing and airing Nazi propaganda.[2]

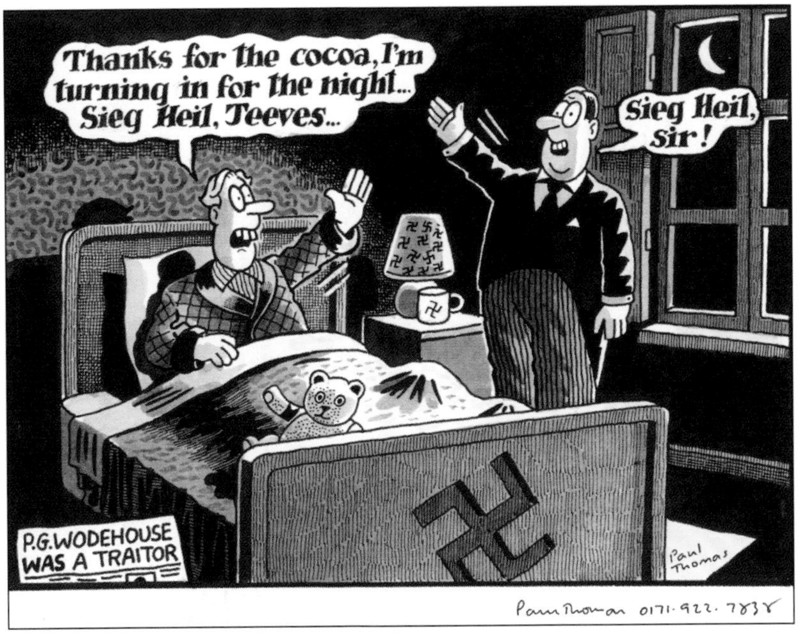
Thanks for the cocoa, I'm turning in for the night... Sieg Heil, Jeeves...
Sieg Heil, Sir!
P.G. WODEHOUSE WAS A TRAITOR
Paul Thomas

While this scandal has largely faded from public consciousness, it was briefly revived in September of 1999 when some British intelligence service documents dealing with Wodehouse's actions were declassified. A 1946 memo stated that Sir Theobald Matthew, director of public prosecutions at the time, felt that Wodehouse should be put on trial for treason if he ever returned to Britain. Wodehouse, however, had already moved to the United States in 1944, and he never returned to Britain.[3] In this cartoon, Thomas shows Bertie and Jeeves giving one another Nazi salutes in a room covered in swastikas.

## 14) INGRAM PINN *Lipstick war*

Ink and watercolor drawing, 23 × 30 cm. / September 13, 2008 / Published in the *Financial Times* (London, England)

While the subject of this cartoon is still widely recognizable, this is an example of a cartoon that will likely be difficult for the average viewer to understand in a few decades.

During Sarah Palin's vice-presidential nomination acceptance speech on September 3rd, 2008, she joked, "The difference between a hockey mom and a pit bull? Lipstick."[2] The remark quickly became one of the most talked-about statements in her speech. On September 9th, 2008, presidential candidate Barack Obama said while discussing rival candidate John McCain's policies, "You can put lipstick on a pig; it's still a pig. You can wrap an old fish in a piece of paper called change; it's still going to stink after eight years." Members of the McCain campaign argued that Obama's use of the phrase "lipstick on a pig" was intended as an insult to McCain's recently announced running mate. Obama's remark and his refusal to apologize led to heated exchanges between the two campaigns.[3]

While Sarah Palin is still a widely recognizable figure, memories of her joke and Obama's subsequent comment are already fading from public consciousness. In several decades, it is possible that Palin, like other vice-presidential candidates who did not make it to the White House, will be difficult for viewers to recognize, and the giant lipstick on which Palin rides will likely be completely baffling to the average viewer.

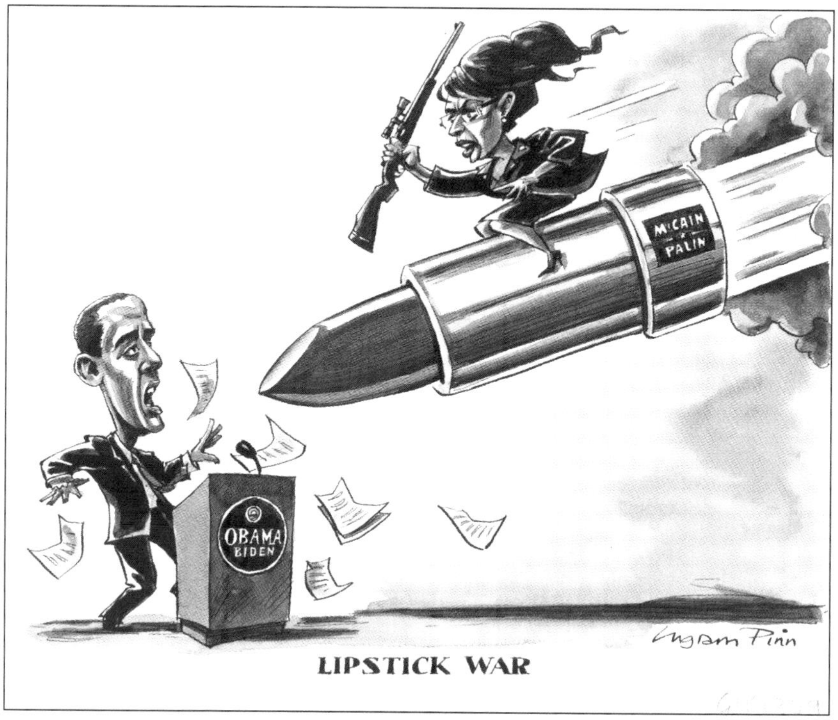
McCAIN - PALIN
OBAMA
BIDEN
Ingram Pinn
LIPSTICK WAR

# II ❦ An Unexpected View of the Well Known

While many political cartoons depict well known or mainstream viewpoints, others depict minority or controversial viewpoints. Additionally, some viewpoints that were common or familiar in the past have become obscure today. When such perspectives are reflected in cartoons, they can often serve as valuable documentation of those views. It can also be illuminating to compare cartoons depicting well known people in expected ways with those depicting them in unexpected ways.

### 15) ADALBERT J. VOLCK ("V. BLADA") *Writing the Emancipation Proclamation*

Etching, 23.7 × 18.2 cm. / 1862 (original design) / Probably published in Baltimore, Maryland

This is one of a series of twenty-nine etchings titled the "Confederate War Etchings" or "Sketches from the Civil War in North America" that Adalbert J. Volck published under the pseudonym V. Blada in 1862. This copy is part of a reissue of the first edition. Volck had immigrated to the United States from Germany, eventually settling in Baltimore, Maryland, where he became a dentist. Despite the fact that Baltimore was controlled by the Union, Volck supported the Confederacy during the Civil War. According to some accounts, he even smuggled supplies and carried messages for the Confederacy. His drawings, however, would have had very limited circulation, even in the North, and they likely were not seen at all in the South until after the war.[1]

President Abraham Lincoln signed the Emancipation Proclamation on January 1st, 1863, granting freedom to slaves in the Confederate States of America. This meant that, as Union troops advanced, slaves in these states would be freed, undermining the Confederacy and strengthening the Union army.[2] This cartoon depicts Lincoln writing the Emancipation Proclamation.

Today, Lincoln is one of the most admired past presidents of the United States, and people today are used to seeing Lincoln depicted as a noble figure. This etching by Volck, however, shows how supporters of the Confederacy viewed Lincoln during the time of the Civil War. His office is decorated with demonic faces, he sits with one foot on a book labeled "U. S. Constitution," and a painting on his wall captioned "St. Do-

mingo" depicts the 1791 to 1793 slave revolt in Haiti (known at the time as Sainte Domingue), which Volck has depicted as a slaughter of women and children. Another painting, captioned "St. Ossawotamie," likely references a battle in Osawatomie, Kansas on August 30, 1856, one of the clashes between pro-slavery and anti-slavery groups during the "Bleeding Kansas" or "Border War" conflict created by the Kansas-Nebraska Act of 1854, which let Kansas voters decide whether the state would be slave or free.[3]

## 16) ADALBERT J. VOLCK ("V. BLADA") *Passage through Baltimore*

Etching, 19 × 11.7 cm. / 1862 (original design) / Probably published in Baltimore, Maryland

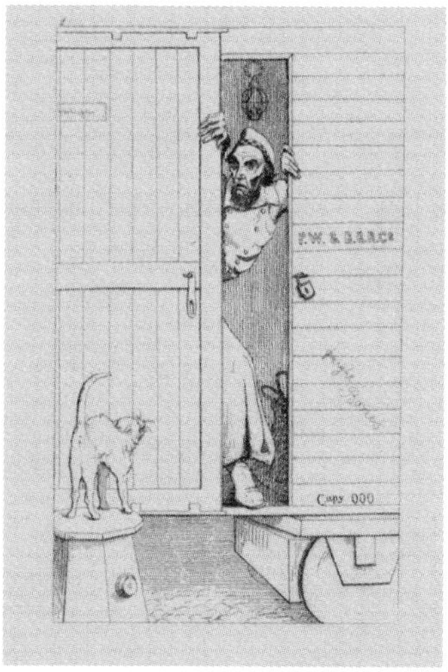

This is another in the series "Confederate War Etchings" by Adalbert Volck.

Like "Writing the Emancipation Proclamation," this cartoon shows Abraham Lincoln in a very unflattering light. It is a reference to the "Baltimore Plot," an incident in which President-elect Lincoln passed through Baltimore secretly in the middle of the night of February 22 to 23, 1861 on his way to his inauguration in Washington D.C. He changed his schedule on the advice of his security manager, Allan Pinkerton, who had evidence that a group of conspirators planned to assassinate Lincoln at his scheduled arrival in Baltimore on February 23, 1861.[1] When it became clear that Lincoln had slipped through Baltimore in secret, many of Lincoln's critics derided his actions as cowardly. The *Baltimore Sun*, for instance, printed "We do not believe the Presidency can ever be more degraded by any of his successors than it has been by him, even before his inauguration."[2]

Volck's cartoon is a similar criticism of Lincoln. Lincoln wears his nightclothes and peers out of the train car in which he is hiding, seemingly terrified by a nearby cat. Volck lived in Baltimore at this time, so he would certainly have known about the controversy surrounding the alleged Baltimore Plot.

## 17) ART YOUNG *Stealing thunder*

Ink drawing, 52 × 34.5 cm. / c. 1901–1909 / Published in *The Coming Nation* (Cave Mills, Tennessee)

In this cartoon, Young shows President Theodore Roosevelt stealing thunder from the socialist cause by providing temporary relief measures, supporting laws that benefit labor, and giving in to some of the socialists' immediate demands. This is a reference to policies Roosevelt pursued as part of his "Square Deal" platform. Roosevelt's position was that the interests of labor and capital had to be balanced and that both should receive fair treatment.

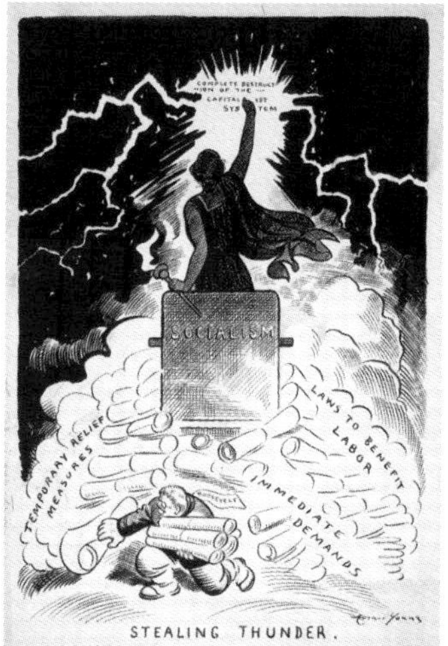
SOCIALISM
TEMPORARY RELIEF MEASURES
LAWS TO BENEFIT LABOR
IMMEDIATE DEMANDS
STEALING THUNDER.
BUT, DONT WORRY, HE WILL NEVER STEAL THE LIGHTNING.

To this end, Roosevelt advocated for the government taking an active role in ensuring that each side dealt fairly with the other. In 1902, Roosevelt mediated the United Mine Workers' strike, which resulted in the workers receiving increased wages and shorter working hours. This was the first time a U.S. president treated both sides in a labor dispute as equals. His administration also filed over forty lawsuits in an attempt to break up trusts, supported the establishment of the Department of Commerce and Labor, and set limits on the rates railroads could charge.[1]

However, Roosevelt's position was more moderate than the socialist Art Young probably would have liked, so Young has shown him weakening the socialist position by supporting reforms to address some of the issues that angered the socialists while leaving the basic structure of capitalism intact. While Roosevelt is remembered as the quintessential progressive president, Young's cartoon shows that not all progressives and reformers were pleased with Roosevelt's actions.

## 18) ART YOUNG [Untitled] *Cartoon of two-faced Woodrow Wilson*

Ink drawing, 22.2 × 21.5 cm. / c. 1919 / Published by *Good Morning* (New York City)

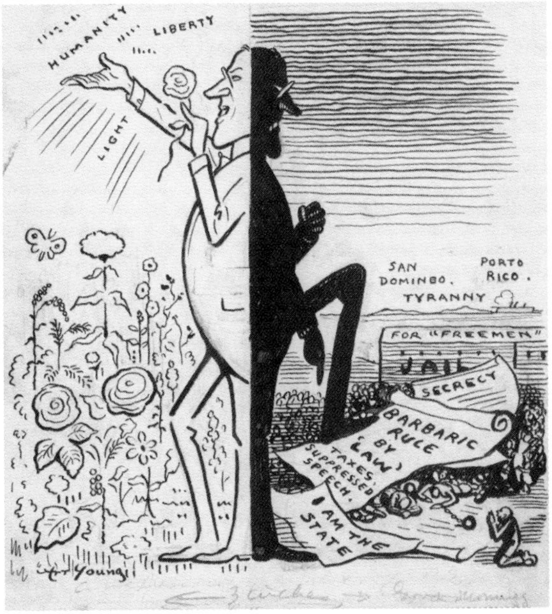
HUMANITY
LIBERTY
LIGHT
SAN DOMINGO.
PORTO RICO.
TYRANNY
FOR "FREEMEN"
JAIL
SECRECY
BARBARIC RULE BY 'LAW'
TAXES, SUPPRESSED SPEECH.
I AM THE STATE
Art Young

Today, President Woodrow Wilson is largely remembered as an advocate for peace. His Fourteen Points speech, his support of the League of Nations, and his receipt of the Nobel Peace Prize are some of the most familiar facts about the twenty-eighth president.[1]

In this cartoon, however, Young shows another side of Wilson. While the left side depicts the peace-loving, progressive Wilson, the right side shows him as a tyrannical ruler. The paper reading "Barbaric rule by 'law'" and "suppressed speech" likely refers to several pieces of unpopular legislation. These included the Selective Service Act of 1917, which instituted the draft; the Espionage Act of 1917, which, in addition to prohibiting the sharing of military information with enemies of the United States, also prohibited any hindering of military recruitment; and the Sedition Act of 1918, which prohibited the publishing of any material calling for an end to the war or any protests against the government which might hinder the war effort. Over one thousand Americans were jailed under the Espionage Act and the Sedition Act.[2]

Young also comments on Wilson's actions in Latin America. On the horizon of the cartoon are islands labeled San Domingo and Puerto Rico with the word tyranny above them. This refers to the eight-year occupation of the Dominican Republic by United States troops that began in 1916 under Wilson's orders, ostensibly to bring stability to the country,[3] and the United States' ongoing relationship with Puerto Rico, which was an unincorporated territory of the United States and treated as a colony. Tensions between the United States and Puerto Rico were heightened by the passage of the Jones Act in 1917, which granted Puerto Ricans U.S. citizenship without making Puerto Rico into a state. With the entry of the United States into World War I appearing increasingly inevitable, this was seen by some as a way of subjecting Puerto Ricans to the draft without giving them a voice in the United States government.[4]

The limits that Wilson's government placed on the activities of its citizens during World War I and United States relations with Latin America under Wilson are not as well remembered today as Wilson's advocacy for peace and a League of Nations, but this cartoon documents a time when many viewed Wilson as little more than a dictator.

## 19) ART YOUNG *The sacred bench*

Ink drawing, 25.5 × 31 cm. / c. 1923 / Publication status unknown

While William Howard Taft is primarily remembered as the twenty-seventh president of the United States (1909–1913), he actually served longer as chief justice of the United States Supreme Court (1921–1930).[1] Young's cartoon refers to this later period of Taft's career.

Specifically, this cartoon is a reference to the $10,000 in interest Taft received annually from bonds he

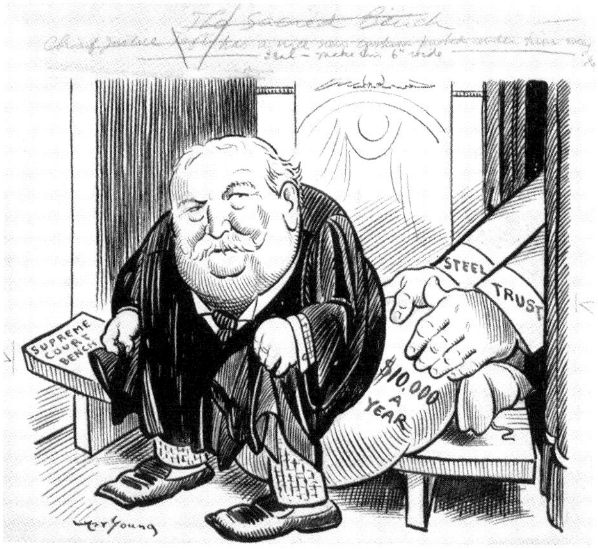
SUPREME COURT BENCH
STEEL TRUST
$10,000 A YEAR

held in the United States Steel Corporation. This was a sizable sum at the time, considering Taft's salary as chief justice was $15,000 a year.[2] This led some people to worry that this powerful corporation was influencing the United States Supreme Court through Taft.[3,4] Young clearly was critical of Taft's acceptance of the money, and he shows the Carnegie "steel trust" padding Taft's seat on the Supreme Court bench. Interestingly, Taft had come under fire from Theodore Roosevelt in 1911 for trying to break up U.S. Steel under the Sherman Antitrust Act of 1890 for anticompetitive behavior in its acquisitions of other companies. The Roosevelt administration and U.S. Steel had shared an understanding that the company would not be subject to antitrust lawsuits for its acquisitions, and Roosevelt felt that Taft had betrayed his trust by taking action against them. This, along with many other factors, led Roosevelt to try to gain the Republican nomination for president over Taft in 1911.[5]

## 20) DANIEL DENNIS *To the rescue!*

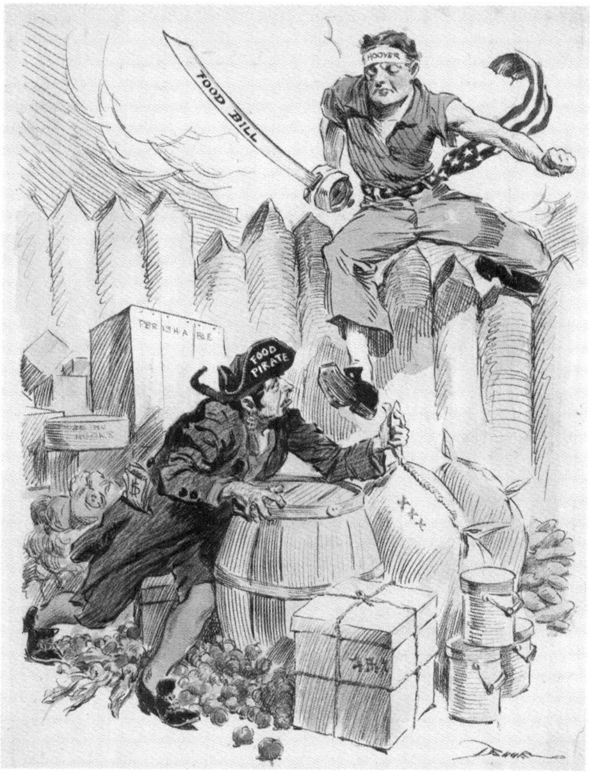
FOOD BILL
HOOVER
FOOD PIRATE
XXX

Ink and watercolor drawing, 48 × 36.5 cm. / c. 1917 / Published in the *Chicago Tribune* (Chicago, Illinois)

Herbert Hoover is frequently vilified for his actions during the Depression, but this cartoon from the front page of the *Chicago Tribune* depicts him at a time before his presidency, when many Americans viewed him as a hero.

After the outbreak of World War I in August 1914, Hoover helped many Americans stranded in Europe return to the United States. He then established the Commission for Relief in Belgium, which supplied food to starving people in German-occupied Belgium and may have saved as many as ten million people from starvation. When the United States entered World War I in 1917, President Wilson appointed Hoover as head of the new United States Food Administration. The Food Administration popularized the slogan "Food Will Win the War" and encouraged Americans to voluntarily conserve food.[1] The "Food Bill" to which the cartoon refers is probably the Lever Food and Fuel Control Act of 1917,[2] legislation which Hoover supported.[3] The Lever Act established the Food Administration and allowed the president to fix the prices of food and fuel to support the war effort.[4] This legislation also curbed the activities of food speculators, who were driving up the price of food.[5]

At the close of World War I, Hoover was one of the most admired people in the world. A *New York Times* poll from 1920 ranked him as one of the ten greatest living Americans. Even future Democratic president Franklin D. Roosevelt wrote of the Republican Hoover, "He is certainly a wonder, and I wish we could make him President of the United States... There could not be a better one."[6] The Hoover in Dennis's cartoon reflects these sentiments: he is young and vigorous, a swashbuckling hero.

All this would change when the Depression struck during Hoover's term as president.

## 21) ART YOUNG *Hoodooed*

Ink and crayon drawing, 23.5 × 24.5 cm. / c. 1933. Published in Art Young and Heywood Broun's *The Best of Art Young,* New York: Vanguard Press, 1936

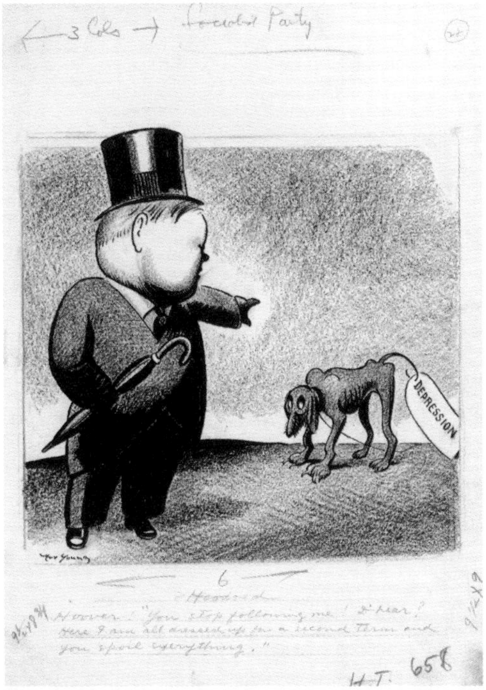
DEPRESSION

Caption: "You stop following me! D'hear. Here I am all dressed up for a second term and you spoil everything."

Modern viewers are more accustomed to the Hoover in Young's cartoon. He is a squat, unromantic figure who wears expensive clothes and tried to escape the Depression that dogs his steps.

Hoover's approach to dealing with the Depression was similar to the one he had employed in organizing his humanitarian efforts: he tried to encourage individual actions and grassroots initiatives. In the case of a massive economic crisis, however, this approach was ineffective, and Hoover quickly became the nation's scapegoat. The shantytowns that appeared around the country were called "Hoovervilles," empty pockets turned inside out were called "Hoover flags," and armadillos, which desperate people sometimes ate, were called "Hoover hogs."[1]

Public ridicule made Hoover's chances at a second term slim, and he was soundly defeated by Franklin D. Roosevelt, who had once said no one could be a better president than Hoover, in the 1932 election.[2]

## 22) FRED O. SEIBEL *"Another tough one to handle"*

Ink and Ben-Day overlay* drawing, 36 × 26 cm. / March 23, 1933 / Published in the *Richmond Times-Dispatch* (Richmond, Virginia)

This cartoon depicts President Franklin D. Roosevelt in a manner that will be familiar to most viewers. The *Richmond Times-Dispatch* published this cartoon just a few weeks into Roosevelt's first hundred days in office, which began on March 4, 1933. During this time, Roosevelt took decisive action to alleviate the Depression that plagued the United States by pushing Congress to pass extensive legislation.[1] This included the Emergency Banking Act, which passed on March 9, 1933 and allowed banks approved by the government to reopen;[2] the Agricultural Adjustment Act, which was submitted to Congress on March 16, 1933[3] and raised the price of food by paying farmers to reduce production;[4] the Economy

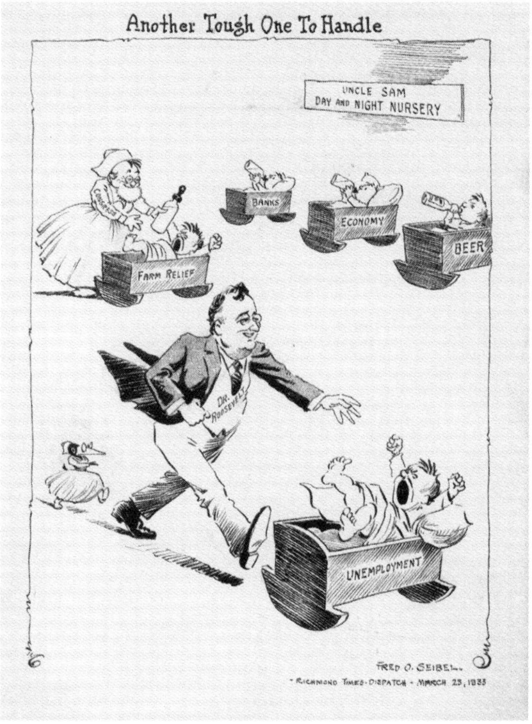
Another Tough One To Handle
UNCLE SAM DAY AND NIGHT NURSERY
BANKS
ECONOMY
BEER
FARM RELIEF
DR. ROOSEVELT
UNEMPLOYMENT
FRED O. SEIBEL
RICHMOND TIMES-DISPATCH - MARCH 23, 1933

ITEM 22

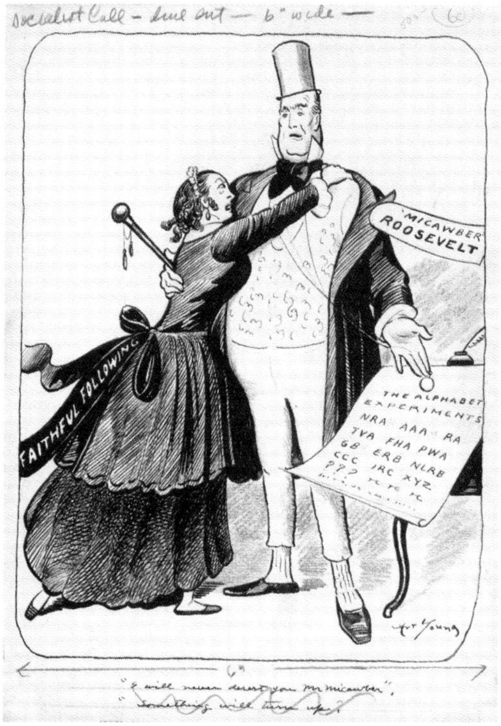
Socialist Call — line cut — 6" wide —
"MICAWBER" ROOSEVELT
FAITHFUL FOLLOWING
THE ALPHABET EXPERIMENTS
NRA AAA RA
TVA FHA PWA
GB ERB NLRB
CCC IRC XYZ
???
Art Young
6"
"I will never desert you Mr Micawber".
"Something will turn up"

ITEM 23

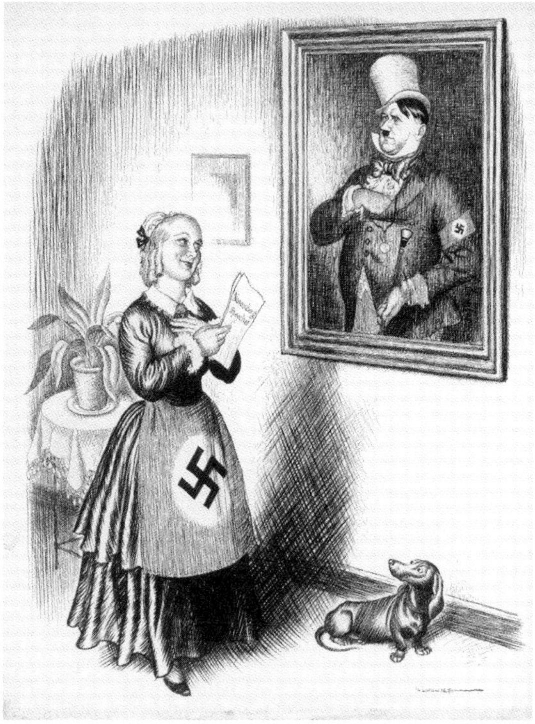

ITEM 24

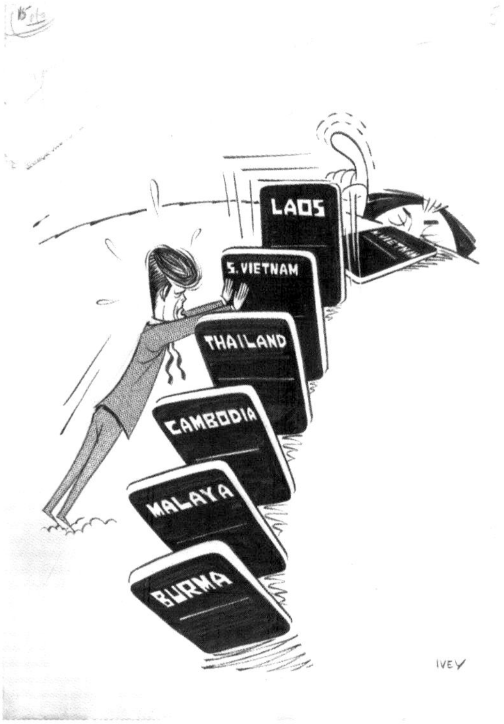
LAOS
S. VIETNAM
THAILAND
CAMBODIA
MALAYA
BURMA
IVEY

ITEM 25

Act, which was enacted on March 20, 1933 and cut the salaries of federal employees and payments to veterans;[5] and the Cullen-Harrison Act, which was signed into law on March 22, 1933[6] and legalized the production of beer with a 3.2% alcohol content.[7]

These and other aspects of Roosevelt's "New Deal" policies are frequently credited with helping to bring the American Depression to an end, and this image of Roosevelt as a doctor ministering to the needs of the nation is similar to the image of the president that has persisted.

*Ben-Day overlays are transparent sheets covered in evenly-spaced dots that some cartoonists use to create shading effects in their drawings. The artist cuts the shape of the shaded area out of the sheet and attaches it to the drawing.

## 23) ART YOUNG *"I will never desert you Mr. Micawber"*

Ink drawing, 33.5 × 25.8 cm. / c. 1939 / Published in *The Nation* (Washington, D.C.)

Unlike Seibel, Young depicts President Franklin D. Roosevelt in a way that is unusual to modern viewers. Here, Young has compared Roosevelt to Wilkins Micawber from Charles Dickens's novel *David Copperfield*, a perpetually destitute character who is convinced that his fortunes will one day turn around and frequently gives others advice. Young has compared the members of the American public who still faithfully follow Roosevelt to Mrs. Micawber, Wilkins Micawber's loyal wife who continues to support him through all his misfortunes and never doubts that his luck will change. She repeatedly says she "will never desert Mr. Micawber."[1] In the cartoon, Roosevelt gestures to a document that lists acronyms of some of the organizations and projects that supported the New Deal, such as the National Recovery Administration, the Agricultural Adjustment Administration, and the Tennessee Valley Authority. Young implies that, just as Micawber's attempts to change his fortune always come to naught, Roosevelt's projects have not brought prosperity to the United States. Nonetheless, Roosevelt and his supporters, like Micawber and his wife, remain perhaps foolishly optimistic that continuing on the same path they have followed in the past will lead them to a different outcome. Young had reason to be skeptical of Roosevelt's ability to turn things around in the United States; in 1929, just before the Depression began, unemployment in the United States was about three percent. In 1933, when the Depression was at its height and Roosevelt entered office, it was just under twenty-five percent. In 1939, around the time Young drew this cartoon, it was still over seventeen percent.[2] Additionally, this high rate of unemployment was at a time when the percentage of the population in the labor force was lower than it is today, since only about twenty-five percent of women worked outside their homes in the 1930s,[3] while today about fifty-eight percent of women participate in the labor force.[4]

This cartoon is interesting not only because it depicts a usually highly regarded president in a negative light, but also because it relies on a literary reference that would be obscure by today's standards. Young, however, clearly expected the reference to be a familiar one to his audience; otherwise, the cartoon could not convey its message effectively.

## 24) LESLIE ILLINGWORTH *Two hearts that beat as one*

Ink drawing, 43 × 33 cm. / September 13, 1937 / Published in *Punch* (London, England)

*Caption:* Frau Germania: "It is evident to me that colonies are the legitimate sphere of action for Herr Micawber."

In this cartoon from 1937, Adolf Hitler, while not depicted in a complimentary fashion, is not yet shown as the monster he would reveal himself to be, and as he was usually depicted, in later years. The caption refers to statements made by Hitler on September 7, 1937 at one of the Nuremburg Rallies. In this speech, Hitler argued that Germany needed to reclaim the colonial possessions it lost after World War I in order to have a secure food supply.[1]

Illingworth's cartoon is also noteworthy in that, like Art Young's cartoon of Roosevelt in "I will never desert you Mr. Micawber" published around the same time (item 23), he has referenced the characters Wilkins Micawber and Mrs. Micawber from Charles Dickens's novel *David Copperfield*.[2] Like Young, Illingworth clearly expects his audience to be acquainted with these characters. In this case, Hitler is depicted as the destitute but optimistic Wilkins Micawber, while his followers are depicted as Micawber's unwaveringly supportive wife who has faith in all her husband's plans, despite his poor track record.

## 25) JIM IVEY *Dominoes*

Ink and Ben-Day overlay* drawing, 28.3 × 23.3 cm. / c. 1963 / Published in the *San Francisco Examiner* (San Francisco, California)

The Vietnam War is frequently associated with the administration of Lyndon B. Johnson, since Johnson initiated the direct involvement of the United States military in the conflict by sending the first U.S. combat troops into South Vietnam in 1965[1] and the antiwar movement became large and vocal during his time as president.[2] United States involvement in the Vietnam War grew significantly under Johnson's predecessor, President John F. Kennedy, however, and this cartoon refers to Kennedy's efforts to prevent South Vietnam from coming under the control of communists. It is a literal depiction of the "Domino Theory" first articulated by President Dwight D. Eisenhower in a speech on April 7, 1954 in which he stated that, if South Vietnam were allowed to become communist, much of the rest of Southeast Asia might follow.[3]

The Kennedy administration provided large amounts of financial aid to the South Vietnamese government to support President Ngo Dinh Diem against his communist enemies, despite the fact that Diem was a corrupt and repressive ruler. Kennedy also increased the number of U.S. military advisors in South Vietnam from 700 to 15,000.[4] This cartoon shows Kennedy attempting to shore up the wobbling domino of South Vietnam. The North Vietnam domino has already fallen before a figure who is probably Chinese communist leader Mao Zedong. Mao prods the domino of Laos, through which the Ho Chi Minh trail ran. This trail served as a supply route and communication line between North Vietnam and communists in South Vietnam.[5] In this cartoon, it is poised to fall and take South Vietnam and the rest of Southeast Asia with it if Kennedy stops providing support to South Vietnam.

## 26) GIB CROCKETT *"Hey!—Looks like somebody's been this way before!"*

Ink and crayon drawing, 33.3 × 31.3 cm. / September 14, 1967 / Published in the *Washington Star* (Washington, D.C.)

Political cartoons serve as particularly interesting documents of their times when they include early depictions of people who went on to become significantly more prominent than they were when the cartoon was created. This cartoon shows Ronald Reagan in 1967, long before he became president of the United States in 1981,[1] but looking much the same as he would in the cartoons of the 1980s.

Reagan became governor of California in 1967, and even as he was just beginning his new role, some of his fellow Republicans were encouraging him to run as the Republican candidate for president.[2] Just three years before, Republican Barry Goldwater had campaigned for president in the 1964 election and

---

*Ben-Day overlays are transparent sheets covered in evenly-spaced dots that some cartoonists use to create shading effects in their drawings. The artist cuts the shape of the shaded area out of the sheet and attaches it to the drawing.

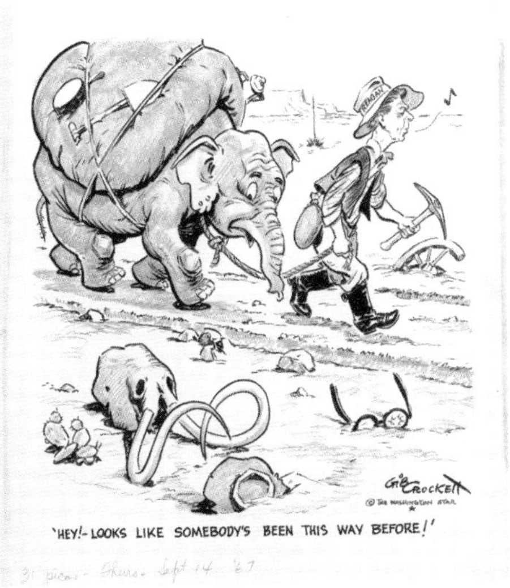
GIB CROCKETT
'HEY!- LOOKS LIKE SOMEBODY'S BEEN THIS WAY BEFORE!'

ITEM 26

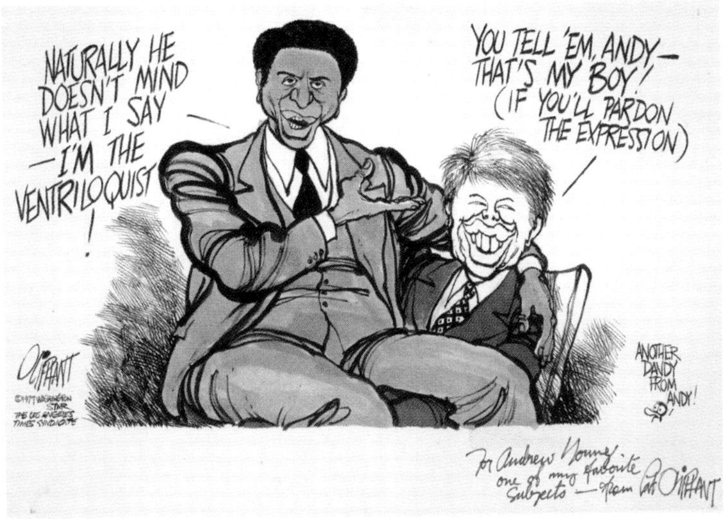
NATURALLY HE DOESN'T MIND WHAT I SAY —I'M THE VENTRILOQUIST!
YOU TELL 'EM, ANDY— THAT'S MY BOY! (IF YOU'LL PARDON THE EXPRESSION)
OLIPHANT
ANOTHER DANDY FROM ANDY!
For Andrew Young one of my favorite subjects — from Pat Oliphant

ITEM 27

was soundly defeated by President Lyndon Johnson.[3] In this cartoon, Crockett shows Reagan whistling obliviously as he leads an elephant, a symbol of the Republican Party, along a path that leads past the skull of an elephant and a broken pair of Goldwater's characteristic glasses. Crockett seems to be suggesting that, if Reagan takes leadership of the Republican Party, he will meet the same fate as Goldwater—defeat. While Reagan would not become the Republican candidate for president until 1980, he would win a decisive victory in that year's election.[4] Ironically, the same year that Reagan became president, the *Washington Star* declared bankruptcy and had to close its doors.[5]

## 27) PAT OLIPHANT *"Naturally, he doesn't mind what I say—I'm the ventriloquist!"*

Ink and watercolor drawing, 28.7 × 41 cm. / April 14, 1977 / Published in the *Washington Star* (Washington, D.C.)

*Caption:* "Naturally he doesn't mind what I say—I'm the ventriloquist!" / "You tell 'em, Andy—that's my boy! (If you'll pardon the expression.)"

Andrew Young was an active leader in the Civil Rights movement. He was a close associate of Dr. Martin Luther King, Jr. and served as executive director of the Southern Christian Leadership Conference. In 1972, he was elected to the U.S. House of Representatives, becoming the first African American to be elected to Congress from Georgia since the Reconstruction era. In 1977, President Jimmy Carter appointed Young U.S. ambassador to the United Nations.[1]

Young was outspoken and independent, and his statements did not always follow State Department policy, sometimes prompting Secretary of State Cyrus Vance to make statements to the effect that Young's personal views did not always reflect the views of the State Department and the Carter administration.[2] This cartoon reflects that situation, showing Young as a dummy on President Carter's knee who, rather than being the expected mouthpiece for the president, is, in fact, the real ventriloquist.

This cartoon also serves as an example of a cartoon that, while not ostensibly about race, makes use of racist imagery and language. This is especially evident in Carter's reference to Young as "boy," a derisive term as used in this context.

Interestingly, this item was once owned by Andrew Young and is inscribed to him by Pat Oliphant.

ITEM 28

GERRY ADAMS
I.R.A
BILL & GERRY
HILARY AND GERRY
TOM & GERRY
WASHINGTON POST
OKLAHOMA HIT BY TERRORIST BOMB
Brook

"JOHN MAJOR WANTS TO REMIND YOU NOT TO FORGET ABOUT THE HANDSHAKE WHEN WE CATCH THEM"

ITEM 29

SCHRANK

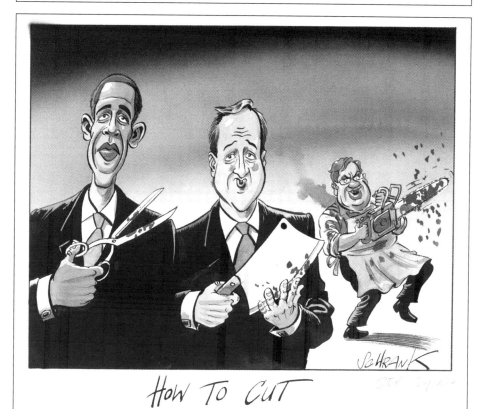

HOW TO CUT

28) RICK BROOKES *"John Major wants to remind you not to forget about the handshake when we catch them"*

Ink drawing, 36 × 47.5 cm. / c. April 19, 1995 / Published in the *Evening Standard* (London, England)

Political cartoons often present a perspective specific to the time and place in which they were created, and this cartoon is a good example of a uniquely British perspective on an American tragedy, the Oklahoma City Federal Building bombing. On April 19, 1995, Timothy McVeigh and Terry Lynn Nichols detonated a bomb outside the Alfred P. Murrah Federal Building in Oklahoma City, killing 168 people.[1] This cartoon places that event within the context of issues which mattered to British audiences.

Gerry Adams joined the Irish Republican Army (IRA) in 1965, eventually becoming one of its leaders. According to some historians, Adams even served as the IRA's chief of staff.[2] The IRA is an organization that seeks to separate Northern Ireland from the United Kingdom and join it and Ireland into a united Ireland. Their tactics include the use of violence, such as on July 21, 1972, a day later dubbed "Bloody Friday," when the organization detonated twenty-six bombs in Belfast, Northern Ireland, killing nine people and wounding many more. Adams may have been involved in this event.[3] The activities of the IRA have led many to consider the group a terrorist organization and Adams a terrorist leader.

The British government and public were unhappy with President Bill Clinton's decision to grant Adams a U.S. visa in 1994, allowing Adams to visit the United States.[4] The first handshake between Clinton and Adams at the U.S. Congress's annual St. Patrick's Day luncheon on March 16, 1995 was also controversial,[5] and this cartoon refers to this incident.

Brookes shows the Oval Office filled with portraits of Adams. A Secret Service agent holds out a phone to Clinton, telling him that British Prime Minister John Major wants to remind Clinton to not forget to shake the hand of the terrorist who has just bombed the Alfred P. Murrah Federal Building when he is caught, just as Clinton shook Adams's hand.

29) PETER SCHRANK *How to Cut*

Ink, airbrush, and watercolor drawing, 20 × 25.5 cm. / October 24, 2010 / Published in the *Sunday Business Post* (Dublin, Ireland)

This is another example of a foreign cartoon in which an American event or public figure is used to comment on an issue important to readers in the country for which the cartoon was created. The cartoonist, Peter Schrank, is Swiss-born,[1] and the cartoon was published in an Irish paper, the *Sunday Business Post*. It would be reasonable to assume that the editors suggested the subject.

This cartoon contrasts the budget cuts by U.S. President Barack Obama and British Prime Minister David Cameron with those by Irish Taoiseach (prime minister) Brian Cowen. This was a reference to Cowen's controversial plans to drastically decrease government spending and increase taxes in an effort to reduce Ireland's budget deficit.[2] After the approval rating of Cowen's party, Fianna Fail, dropped to eight percent as a result of his actions, he resigned as head of the party in January 2011 and did not run in the next general election in February 2011.[3] While Obama and Cameron's budget cuts were controversial in their own countries, in this cartoon they are depicted as much more reasonable than Cowen's plans.

# III Prejudice and Stereotypes

Political art frequently includes stereotypical or prejudiced depictions of particular groups of people. The items in this group make use of stereotypes in ways that are particularly revealing of the attitudes in the times and places in which they were created.

## A. GENERAL

This section contains cartoons that reflect a variety of racial, religious, and gender stereotypes.

### 30) ART YOUNG *"You're a liar—I didn't eat no wahtermelon—deed I didn't"*

Ink and crayon drawing, 33.5 × 31 cm. / September 10, 1912 / Published in *Puck* (New York City)

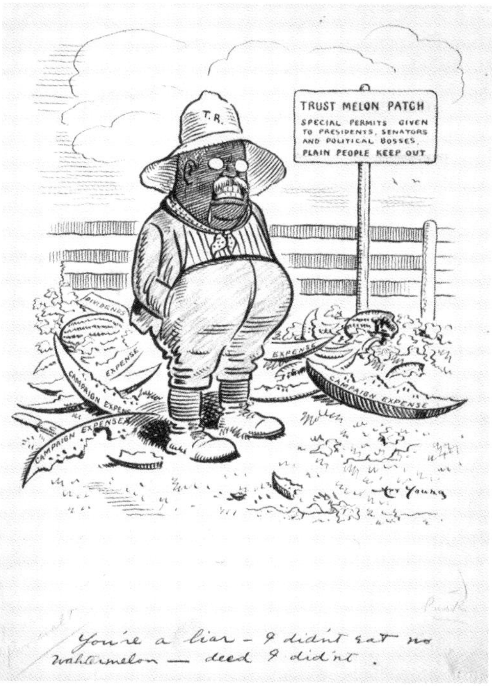
TRUST MELON PATCH
SPECIAL PERMITS GIVEN TO PRESIDENTS, SENATORS AND POLITICAL BOSSES.
PLAIN PEOPLE KEEP OUT
T.R.
DIVIDENDS
EXPENSE
CAMPAIGN EXPENSE
Art Young
You're a liar - I didn't eat no wahtermelon — deed I didn't.

This drawing shows how cartoonists sometimes casually used extremely racist imagery in works that ostensibly had nothing to do with race. In this cartoon, Young has depicted former President Theodore Roosevelt as an African American man and used the stereotype that African Americans are fond of watermelon[1] as a metaphor for Roosevelt's behavior.

In 1912, Roosevelt, who was unhappy with President William Howard Taft's administration, split from the Republican Party and founded the Progressive, or Bull Moose, Party. At the time of this cartoon, Roosevelt was running for president as a third party candidate.[2] This cartoon probably refers to the controversy that emerged in 1912 over campaign funds Roosevelt had received in 1904. Senator Boies Penrose, who was a member of the Republican National Executive Committee and chairman of the New York Republican State Committee, had received a $25,000 check from John D. Archbold of the Standard Oil Company. In August of 1912, when Penrose was under investigation, he stated that the money went towards Roosevelt's campaign in New York, and that it assisted Roosevelt in carrying New York in the 1904 election.[3] Ultimately, it emerged that both Standard Oil and J. P. Morgan had contributed to Roosevelt's 1904 campaign. In testimony before a Senate investigating committee on October 4, 1912, Roosevelt denied that he had any knowledge of these contributions. He also denied that anyone received favors for contributing to his campaign.[4]

In this cartoon, Young seems skeptical of Roosevelt's innocence. The fact that he has used a racial stereotype of African Americans to comment on Roosevelt's behavior reveals how pervasive and unquestioned these stereotypes were at the time. Young is also echoing the image, common at the time, of African Americans stealing watermelons from watermelon patches. Additionally, he is drawing on racist notions that African Americans were simple-minded or child-like[5] by depicting Roosevelt as a black man denying that he has eaten any watermelon when he is obviously surrounded by rinds. That a cartoonist like Art Young, who considered himself open-minded and identified as a socialist,[6] would use a racial stereotype in this way is particularly revealing of how entrenched racism was in the United States at this time.

## 31) C. N. ROMANOS *The black dictator*

Ink drawing, 15 × 19 cm. / 1941 / Published in *The Sphinx* (Egypt)

*Caption:* "I want it served sautéed." / "But your highness, fascism is served water-boiled."

This cartoon was drawn by a Greek cartoonist working for a publication in Egypt during the time of the Second World War. It depicts Italian dictator Benito Mussolini as Romanos's idea of an African tribal leader and a cannibal. Like Art Young in his cartoon of Theodore Roosevelt, Romanos is drawing on racist imagery in a cartoon that is not about race relations in order to criticize a political figure. Romanos intends to suggest that Mussolini is barbaric or primitive by depicting him as an African leader, qualities Romanos expected his audience would associate with these cultures.

The Greeks had reason to dislike Mussolini, since Greece was occupied by the Axis powers in April of 1941 and divided into zones of control managed by Italy, Germany, and Bulgaria.[1]

## 32) ARTHUR SZYK *And what would you do with Hitler?*

Ink and pencil drawing, 14 × 23 cm. / 1944 / Published in Arthur Szyk and Maxwell Struthers Burt's *Ink and Blood: A Book of Drawings,* New York: The Heritage Press, 1946

*Caption:* "And what would you do with Hitler?" / "I would have made him a Negro, and dropped him somewhere in the U.S.A...."

In this cartoon, the artist directly criticizes racism towards African Americans in the United States. Even so, the image is problematic by today's standards.

During the World War II era, African Americans faced significant discrimination. Jim Crow laws were in full force, and even areas without such laws were heavily segregated. Initially, African Americans were underrepresented in the military because of pervasive, racist notions that they were cowardly and disloyal. The 1940 Selective Service Act, however, placed large numbers of African Americans in combat positions, and by September of 1944, African Americans comprised 8.7% of the men serving.[1] While this change represented some progress, combat units were still segregated and African American soldiers often did not receive the same recognition for their service that white soldiers did. This led African American newspapers to coin the term "Double V Campaign," victory over fascism abroad and victory over racism at home, to refer to the struggles of African American citizens during this time.[2]

In this item, an African American soldier comments to a white soldier that turning Nazi leader Adolf

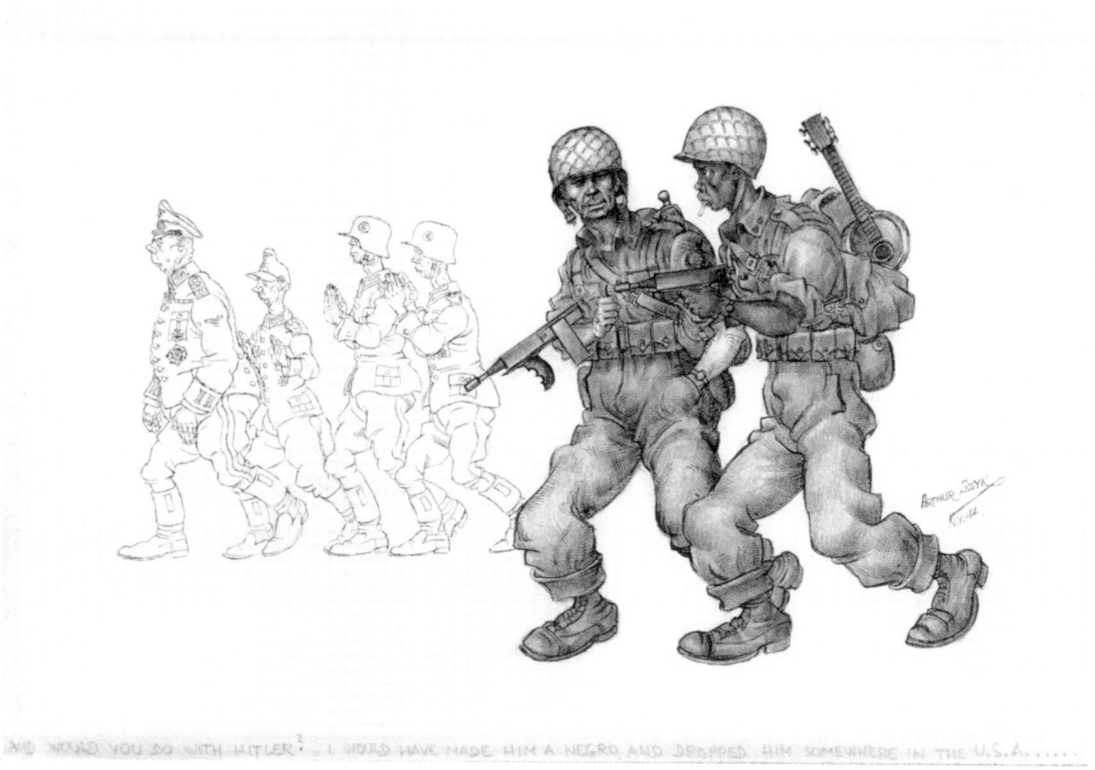
WOULD YOU DO WITH HITLER? .. I WOULD HAVE MADE HIM A NEGRO AND DROPPED HIM SOMEWHERE IN THE U.S.A. ....

Hitler into a black man and dropping him into the United States would be a fitting punishment. Clearly, Szyk is criticizing the conditions faced by African Americans in the United States. Szyk, who was Polish-born, was often critical of racism towards African Americans, and he was especially sympathetic to the plight of black veterans.[3] Even so, Szyk has, perhaps unconsciously, relied on some racist stereotypes in his drawing. The African American soldier is drawn in a more cartoonish style than the white soldier, and his facial features are slightly exaggerated. Additionally, the African American soldier carries a banjo in his pack, and the banjo-playing African American was a common racial stereotype.[4] The fact that Szyk, who seems to have been legitimately passionate about combating racism towards African Americans, would make use of racist imagery shows how ingrained these attitudes were, even in a liberal immigrant like Szyk.

## 33) L. M. GLACKENS *At the Bohemian Club*

Ink and crayon drawing, 30.5 × 41.7 cm. / May 17, 1911 / Published in *Puck* (New York City)

Glackens drew this cartoon in 1911, when women were becoming increasingly involved in politics and other concerns outside the home and the women's suffrage movement was gaining traction. These activities raised anxieties among many people about women's changing roles in society.

The 1912 election, which was held just a year and a half after this cartoon was published, was noteworthy for being the first in which women played a significant role. In this election, women organized in large numbers to support some of the causes of the Progressive Movement and women's suffrage became a national issue.[1] Women's clubs that focused on self-improvement had been common since the mid-19$^{th}$ century, but during the Progressive Era, increasing numbers of women's clubs began taking up social reform causes.[2] Additionally, the term feminism came into common use after about 1910 to describe the movement among some women for not only women's suffrage, but full economic and social equality with men. This movement was strongly associated with the bohemians of New York's Greenwich Village.[3] During this period, the word "bohemian" was used to describe people who lived unconventional lifestyles and dedicated themselves to the arts.[4]

Many Americans resisted these changes. For instance, the National Association Opposed to Woman Suffrage was founded in 1911,[5] and by 1915 it had over 200,000 members. Women demonstrating in support of women's rights were sometimes even subjected to physical violence by onlookers.[6]

This cartoon reflects the discomfort Glackens and others felt with women taking on roles other than their traditional ones as caretakers within the home. Glackens has used inverted gender stereotypes to mock the women who were striving for a greater voice in society and the men who supported them.

In the drawing, men and women socialize in the "Bohemian Club," an inversion of the elite social clubs of the time that were usually only open to men.[7] Not only are women present in this usually male space, but they have taken on the qualities traditionally associated with men while the men have taken on qualities traditionally associated with women. The women all have more imposing physical presences than the men and wear masculine clothing, while the men are smaller, adopt more submissive postures, and wear clothing  with more ornaments and frills than the women's. Glacken's implication is that women are attempting to usurp the roles of men, and his drawing is intended to show how ridiculous such a world would be. In doing so, he reveals what behaviors and physical attributes he expected his audience to consider natural for men and women.

## 34) LINLEY E. SAMBOURNE *Turkey and Russia*

Ink drawing, 28 × 23 cm. / August 22, 1896 / Published in *Punch* (London, England)

This cartoon probably comments on the Armenian Massacres of 1894 to 1896 in the Ottoman Empire, in which between 100,000 and 300,000 Armenians were killed by Turkish forces. These massacres are usually called the Hamidian massacres, after Abdul Hamid II, the reigning sultan at the time,[1] who may have ordered them.[2]

Sambourne depicts Abdul Hamid II, who considered himself a modernizer,[3] in a style of traditional clothing his audience would have associated with the Turks, but which is not an accurate reflection of what he would have worn. This clothing is blood stained, and the sultan waves a bloody sword above his head. A bear, a traditional symbol of Russia, looks on like an indulgent parent. Russia exerted a great deal of influence in Turkey during this time,[4] and the Russian government would not intervene on

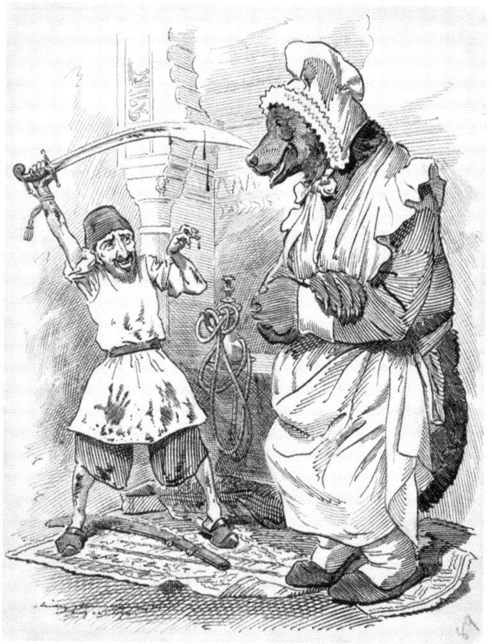

behalf of the Armenians,[5] nor would it allow any other government to do so.[6] Some believed that Russia's government was deliberately exacerbating Turkey's interior conflicts to weaken the Empire and bring it more fully under Russian domination.[7]

The depiction of Abdul Hamid II in this cartoon is particularly interesting in comparison to C. N. Romanos's cartoon "The Black Dictator" (item 31) and Ed Gunder's "Ancient Barbarism" (item 44). Romanos's cartoon depicts Italian dictator Benito Mussolini as a stereotypical, primitive African leader and Gunder's cartoon depicts Japanese Emperor Hirohito's shadow as a stereotypical, primitive Japanese figure. While Sambourne's cartoon is from a very different time period than Romanos's and Gunder's cartoons and Romanos is from a very different cultural background than Sambourne and Gunder, it is interesting to note that when Romanos wants to portray a Western leader as a primitive savage, he depicts him as a member of a non-Western culture, while when Sambourne and Gunder seek to portray their non-Western subjects as primitive savages, they depict their subjects as stereotypical, primitive members of their own cultures. This seems to suggest that these cartoonists considered non-Western appearances a convenient visual shorthand for barbarism.

## 35) C. N. ROMANOS [Untitled] *Cartoon of Roosevelt and Jewish figures*

Ink drawing, 14 × 24.3 cm. / 1939 / Published in *The Sphinx* (Egypt)

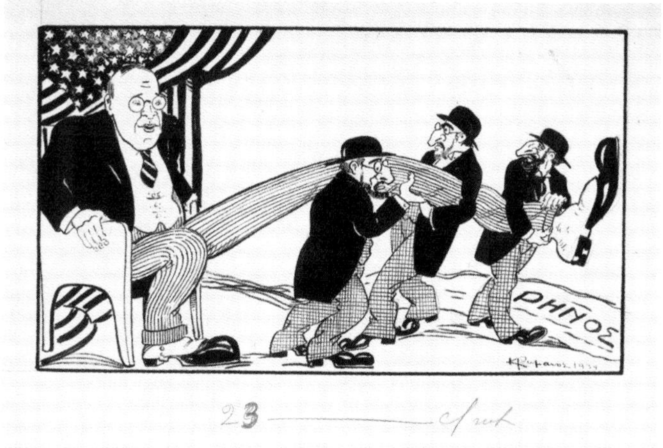
ΡΗΝΟΣ

This drawing, which was published in *The Sphinx*, a Greek-language, Egyptian periodical, includes examples of anti-Semitic figures. Romanos depicts three figures with facial features and clothes associated with anti-Semitic stereotypes of Jews pulling U.S. President Franklin D. Roosevelt's foot over a river labeled "Rhine" in Greek. This could be a reference to accusations by the Italian[1] and German[2] governments that Roosevelt was adopting a less neutral position on the war in Europe at the behest of Jewish-American agitators. Both criticized Roosevelt in July of 1939 for urging the Senate to overturn the House's decision to impose an embargo on the shipment of arms to all nations at war, which he argued would increase the chances of the U.S. being drawn into World War II.[3] This could also be a reference to Roosevelt's support of the Zionist movement.[4]

In either case, Romanos has depicted the Jewish figures in his cartoon in a stereotypical fashion and seems to be suggesting that they are manipulating Roosevelt's actions. While none of Romanos's cartoons are sympathetic to the Axis powers, who would invade Romanos's native Greece in 1940,[5] this cartoon reveals generally accepted anti-Semitic attitudes. This cartoon may reflect prevalent attitudes in the Greek-Egyptian community of which Romanos was a member.

## 36) H. STRICKLAND CONSTABLE [Untitled] *Profiles of Aboriginal Irish Celt, Sir Isaac Newton, and Negro*

Book illustration / *What Science is Saying about Ireland*, Kingston-upon-Hull: Lang and Co., 1881

ABORIGINAL IRISH CELT.
SIR ISAAC NEWTON.
NEGRO.


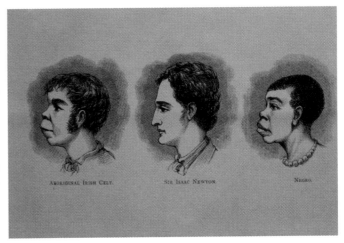

This book puts forward what the author describes as scientific evidence of the inferiority of the Irish to the English, which he uses as a justification for England's continued rule over Ireland. It contains an illustration that purports to show the profiles of an "Aboriginal Irish Celt," "Sir Isaac Newton" (who is intended to represent the Englishman), and a "Negro." The features of the "Aboriginal Irish Celt" and the "Negro" are shown to be similar, while Isaac Newton has very different facial features.

Since racism directed towards the Irish and the stereotypes used to represent them are likely to be less familiar to modern American viewers than some of the other examples of prejudice elsewhere in this exhibit, I have included this item to provide context for the cartoons that include Irish stereotypes. In this image, the artist is clearly drawing parallels between the appearances of the Irish and African figures. This is doubly revealing of the artist's racist attitudes, since it shows not only that he intended to depict the Irish as inferior to the English, but also that he considered people of African descent to be so evidently inferior to the English that he sought to "prove" the Irish were also inferior to the English by drawing parallels between the two.

The notion that there was scientific evidence that some races were superior to others was common in the 19th century, and it was particularly common for English writers and thinkers of the time to consider the Irish less evolved than Anglo-Saxons. In the cartoons of the day, the Irish were frequently portrayed with ape-like features, reflecting the view that the Irish were primitive and undeveloped.[1]

The same image was published in the magazine *Harper's Weekly* in 1899 with the images captioned "Irish Iberian," "Anglo-Teutonic," and "Negro." It also included the following caption: "The Iberians are believed to have been originally an African race, who thousands of years ago spread themselves through Spain over Western Europe... The skulls are of low prognathous type. They came to Ireland and mixed with the natives of the South and West, who themselves are supposed to have been of low type and descendants of savages of the Stone Age, who, in consequence of isolation from the rest of the world, had never been out-competed in the healthy struggle of life, and thus made way, according to the laws of nature, for superior races."[2] The artist is clearly suggesting that the English are one of these "superior races."

## 37) THOMAS NAST *The ignorant vote—honors are easy*

Tear sheet, 36.8 × 24.3 cm. / December 9, 1876 / Published in *Harper's Weekly* (New York City)

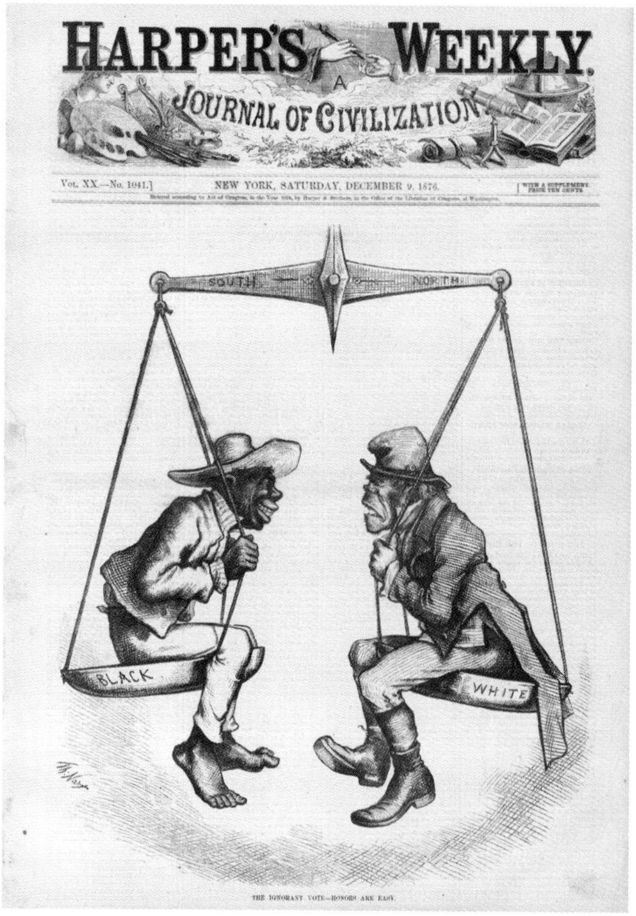
HARPER'S WEEKLY
A JOURNAL OF CIVILIZATION
Vol. XX.—No. 1041.]
NEW YORK, SATURDAY, DECEMBER 9, 1876.
SOUTH
NORTH
BLACK
WHITE
THE IGNORANT VOTE—HONORS ARE EASY.

This item is an example of a cartoon that uses stereotypes in both an Irish figure and an African American figure. The subject of the cartoon is the disputed presidential election of 1876. The Republican candidate, Rutherford B. Hayes, won 165 electoral votes; the Democratic candidate, Samuel J. Tilden, won 184 electoral votes; and 20 electoral votes were disputed. Three of the four states in which the returns were disputed were Florida, Louisiana, and South Carolina. All three were under Reconstruction governments supervised by the Republican federal government, and the official returns from those states gave Hayes the election, while local election officials, who were Democrats, gave Tilden the election. Congress created a special electoral commission to investigate the disputed returns, and the commission ultimately awarded all four states to Hayes.[1] There were rumors that the Democrats and Republicans in Congress struck a deal whereby the Democrats would allow Hayes to become president without protest if Hayes ended Reconstruction. This rumored deal was called the Compromise of 1877.[2] Hayes did ultimately end Reconstruction during his term.[3]

In this image, Nast shows an African American and an Irish American seated on opposite sides of a scale. The bar of the scale above the African American is labeled "South" while the one over the Irish American is labeled "North." Both figures have stereotypically exaggerated facial features. The African American figure, for instance, has the wide lips frequently used in racist caricatures of African Americans.[4] The Irish American figure has the simian appearance and a jutting jaw typical of racist caricatures of the Irish.[5] These features alone are enough to reveal that the artist intends this figure to represent an Irish American, but the clay pipe in his hatband also clearly marks him as an Irishman.[6]

The two figures are in balance, showing that they are equal. Given the title of the piece, Nast intends to show that they are equally ignorant. African American men had received the right to vote with the passage of the 15th Amendment in 1870, just six years before Nast drew this cartoon.[7] Nast is suggesting that the ignorant votes by African Americans in the South for Republicans will balance the ignorant votes by Irish Americans in the North for Democrats.[8] Like Constable (item 36), he is comparing the two groups to one another and dehumanizing both.

## 38) BERNHARD GILLAM *Democracy's Dilemma*

Ink drawing, 25.5 × 13.5 cm. / May 9, 1883 / Published in *Puck* (New York City)

This cartoon refers to the "tariff question," the controversy over the Tariff of 1883, which President Chester A. Arthur signed into law on March 3, 1883. This tariff was sometimes called the "Mongrel Tariff"[1] since it modified tariff rates inconsistently and seemingly arbitrarily, raising rates on some goods and lowering them on others. The legislation was also very complex.[2]

Republicans supported "protectionism," which means they favored high tariffs to protect American industry.[3] Democrats, on the other hand, favored lower tariffs to lower the price on goods.[4] Overall, this tariff was a victory for protectionism, since it lowered tariffs an average of less than two percent, while President Arthur had advocated for reductions of twenty to twenty-five percent.[5]

In this cartoon, Gillam depicts a figure with the ape-like features stereotypically associated with the Irish[6] in a "no policy" tree, avoiding the slavering, "tariff question" bear. Since the Irish were strongly associated with the Democratic Party at this time, especially in New York,[7] where this cartoon was published, Gillam is probably commenting on the Democrats' failure to achieve greater reductions in the tariff.

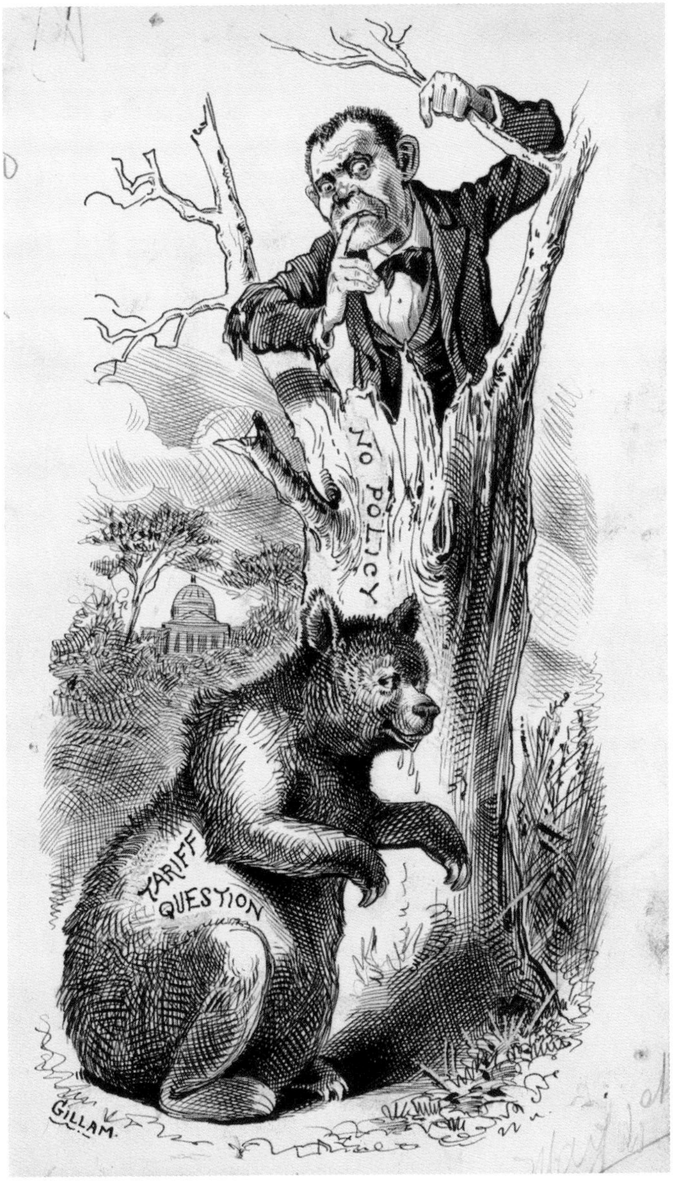
NO POLICY
TARIFF QUESTION
GILLAM.

## B. ASIAN

The items in this section show many facets of the complex and problematic ways in which cartoonists may use similar stereotypes within different contexts and to different ends. These items have been selected for the ways in which they illuminate one another and they are described in relation to one another.

### 39) KOBAYASHI KIYOCHIKA *A thick-skinned face*

Color woodblock print, 35 × 24 cm. / From the series *Hurrah for Japan: One Hundred Selections, One Hundred Laughs* / February 1895 / Published by Matsuki Heikichi (Tokyo, Japan)

This Japanese color print is part of a series titled "Hurrah for Japan: One Hundred Selections, One Hundred Laughs," a collection of propagandistic images of the First Sino-Japanese War, which lasted from 1894 to 1895. During this conflict, Japan fought China for control of Korea and emerged victorious, establishing itself as a major power in East Asia.[1] During this conflict, Japanese artists were very active, producing more than three thousand images of the war in less than a year.[2] Kiyochika was trained in Western artistic techniques by Charles Wirgman,[3] producer of the popular periodical *Japan Punch*,[4] and the composition of

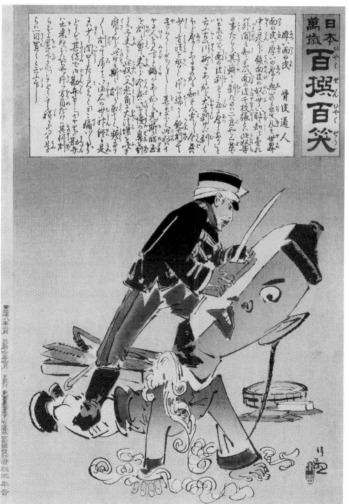

this print shows a fusion of Western and Japanese styles. Kiyochika's style is distinctive, and his prints of the First Sino-Japanese War are sometimes considered a precursor to modern manga.[5] The smooth gradations of the color in the print demonstrate the refinement of printing techniques in Japan at this time.

This artist has set up the Japanese and Chinese figures in sharp contrast to one another. He has depicted the Chinese figure in an exaggerated, stereotypical fashion, with features like the traditional garb and braid highlighted and the figure's face exaggerated to cartoonish proportions. The Japanese figure, on the other hand, is depicted in a more realistic style and is shown in a Western-style uniform, a choice that reflects the enthusiasm for Westernization in Meiji-era Japan[6] and the eagerness of the Japanese to identify with Western societies while distancing themselves from other Asian societies.[7]

## 40) BERNHARD GILLAM *An act forbidding Chinese immigration*

Ink drawing, 19 × 23 cm. / 1882 / Published in *Puck* (New York City)

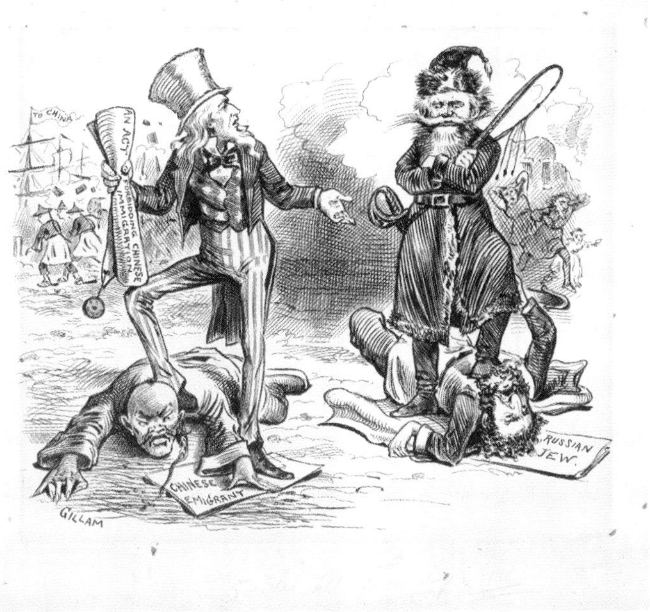
TO CHINA
AN ACT FORBIDDING CHINESE IMMIGRATION
CHINESE EMIGRANT
RUSSIAN JEW
GILLAM

In this drawing, well-known American cartoonist Bernhard Gillam comments on the hypocrisy of Americans and the U.S. government for criticizing the anti-Jewish pogroms in the Russian Empire,[1] which broke out after the assassination of Tsar Alexander II and lasted from 1881 to 1882,[2] while discriminating against the Chinese by banning all immigration to the United States through the Chinese Exclusion Act. This act, which banned all Chinese immigration to the United States for ten years,[3] was signed into law by President Chester A. Arthur on May 6, 1882.[4] It was renewed for another ten years in 1892[5] and signed into law by President Benjamin Harrison.[6] In 1902, it was renewed indefinitely.[7] The ban was supported by groups like the American Federation of Labor, which even sought to extend the restriction to also cover all Japanese immigrants.[8] American sentiment towards the Chinese finally began to shift during World War II, when the United States and China were allies. The Chinese Exclusion Act was repealed in 1943, after more than sixty years of enforcement.[9]

While Gillam's attitude may have been relatively progressive for the time, his heavily stereotyped figure representing a Chinese-American immigrant, which is very similar to the Chinese figure in Kiyochika's print (item 39), shows that even such defenders of Chinese immigrants still had a long way to go.

## 41) HOWLETT *Decorating China*

Ink drawing, 13.3 × 22 cm. / 1910 / Publication status unknown

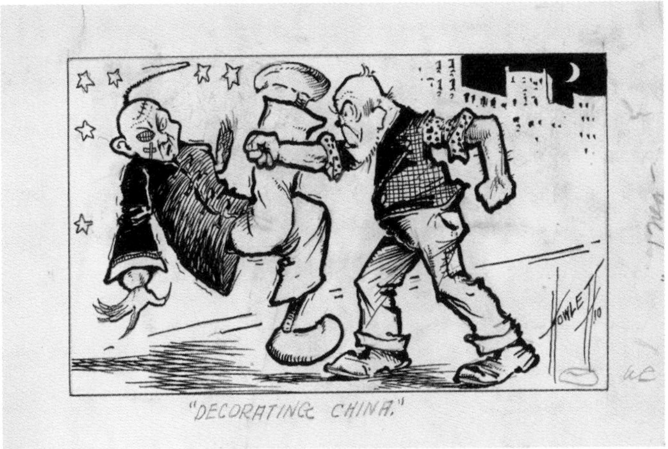
HOWLETT 10
"DECORATING CHINA."

This small drawing is another example of an American cartoonist's use of a stereotypical Chinese-American figure. In addition, the thuggish figure punching the Chinese figure is an example of an Irish-American stereotype.[1] The artist seems to be ridiculing both groups.

## 42) OTHO CUSHING *I am his Uncle Sam*

Ink drawing, 33 × 35.5 cm. / August 3, 1911 / Published in *Life* (New York City)

This item is a commentary on the Currency Reform and Industrial Development Loan, a massive loan by American, British, French, and German banks that was accepted by the Chinese government on May 9, 1911.[1] This loan is an example of the "Dollar Diplomacy" approach towards foreign relations by the United States during this time.[2] The Japanese and Russian governments later wanted to participate in this loan,[3] with the Japanese government claiming that the American government was only supporting the loan in an effort to obtain a more favorable political position in China at the expense of Japan and Russia.[4]

This item, drawn roughly twenty years after Kiyochika's print (item 39) was made, shows that, while the Japanese may have been embracing aspects of Western culture, choosing to adopt Western dress, and highlighting the non-Western appearance of their enemies in order to ridicule them, Western artists did not necessarily see the Japanese in the same way. In this image, Cushing has depicted a Japanese figure in traditional samurai armor. While this depiction may not be as clear an attempt at ridicule as is the traditional clothing in Kiyochika's print, it illustrates that Cushing knew that his audience would quickly identify the figure as Japanese based on the exaggerated and outdated costume.

This cartoon also contains an elaborate literary reference. The drawing includes a parody (see below) of Samuel Taylor Coleridge's poem "Rime of the Ancient Mariner" pasted on the back. It is unclear whether this text was included with the published version. Cushing clearly expected his audience to be familiar with the language and cadence of the poem.

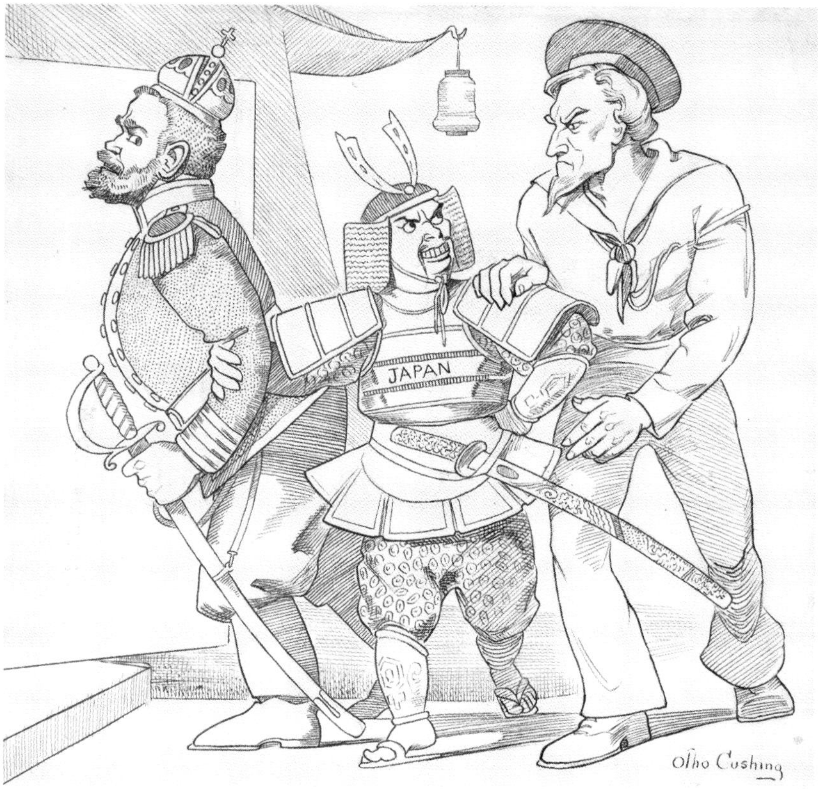
JAPAN
Otho Cushing

May 9, 1911

A TALE OF THE CHINA SEIZE

It is an ancient mariner
Who stoppeth one of two—
"Hold off, unhand me greybeard loon
Pray who the deuce are you?
The Dragon's door is open wide
And we are next of kin.
The guests are met, the feast is set—
But where do you come in?"
He holds them with his Eagle eye,
Then answers like a lamb:
"I am the Dragon's uncle, boys,
I am his Uncle Sam.
(An "uncle" who can make a loan
Stands very near the Dragon's throne)
And that is what I am."
The wedding guests here beat their breasts
It was an awful bore
To hear the claim of Uncle Sam
(For which they did not care a ——)
At China's Open Door.

Compare to the opening lines of the original:

It is an ancient mariner,
And he stoppeth one of three:
'By thy long grey beard and glittering eye,
Now wherefore stopp'st thou me?
The bridegroom's doors are opened wide,
And I am next of kin;
The guests are met, the feast is set—
Mayst hear the merry din.'
He holds him with his skinny hand,
'There was a ship,' quoth he;
'Hold off! unhand me, grey-beard loon!'
Eftsoons his hand dropt he.
He holds him with his glittering eye—
The wedding-guest stood still,
And listens like a three years' child:
The Mariner hath his will.[5]

## 43) HANPER *Japan getting right before the world*

Ink drawing, 46 × 40 cm. / c. 1935 / Publication status unknown

This piece by Hanper comments on Japan's attempt in the mid-1930s to turn the five northern China provinces of Hebei, Chahar, Suiyuan, Shanxi, and Shandong into "autonomous" states with the intention of setting up puppet governments controlled by Japan.[1]

While this piece was drawn roughly fifty years after Gillam's, it is similarly problematic. While it is ostensibly sympathetic to the Chinese, who are represented by a figure held at gunpoint by Japanese figures, the Chinese figure is even more heavily stereotyped than the Japanese figures. The artist has drawn on racist caricatures in his depiction of the two Japanese soldiers, but his Chinese figure still has much in common with those of Kiyochika, Gillam, and Howlett.

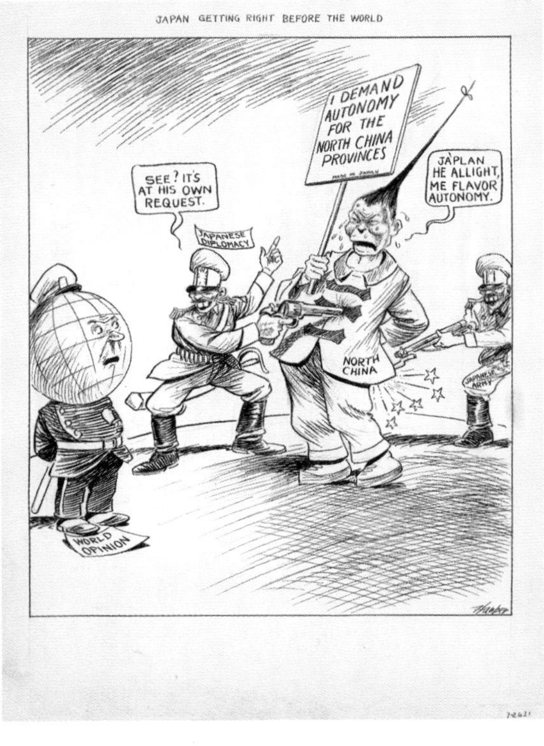
JAPAN GETTING RIGHT BEFORE THE WORLD
I DEMAND AUTONOMY FOR THE NORTH CHINA PROVINCES
SEE? IT'S AT HIS OWN REQUEST.
JAPANESE DIPLOMACY
JAPLAN HE ALLIGHT, ME FLAVOR AUTONOMY.
NORTH CHINA
JAPANESE ARMY
WORLD OPINION

## 44) ED GUNDER *Ancient barbarism*

Ink drawing, 50 × 43 cm. / 1944 / Published by the American Press Association

In this piece, created at the height of the conflict between the United States and Japan during World War II, Gunder has, like the other artists, used clothing as a means of showing the ridiculed figure to be a primitive "other." While the Japanese figure wears Western-style clothing, he kneels before a flaming altar that casts his shadow behind him. This shadow, which carries a sword and wears non-Western clothing, seems to represent the true nature of the figure, and it is his Western clothing that is the costume.

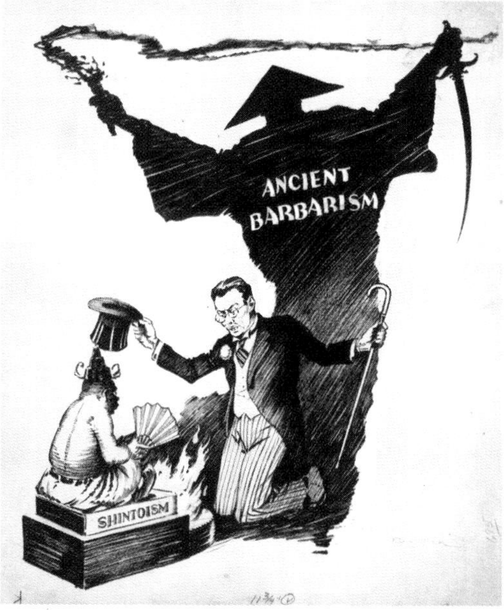
ANCIENT BARBARISM
SHINTOISM

## 45) C. N. ROMANOS *The Involuntary Harakiri*

Ink drawing, 12 × 12.5 cm. / 1942 / Published in *The Sphinx* (Egypt)

This drawing, which was published in Egypt in a Greek-language periodical, *The Sphinx*, shows another variation on the theme of the use of stereotypical traditional clothing as a means of ridicule. In this image, a figure representing Japan is kicked by the Axis powers onto the sword of the United States, referring to the Pacific theater of World War II. In this case, the central figure is intended to represent Japan, but the artist has clearly conflated China and Japan and has dressed the figure in a representation of traditional Chinese clothing.

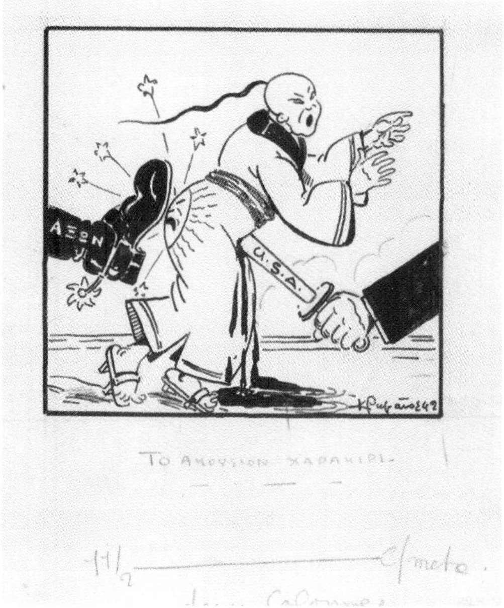
U.S.A.

# IV ❦ Cultural Touchstones

Cartoonists frequently make references to people, images, and stories with which they know their audiences will be familiar. Use of familiar cultural touchstones that have well-established associations allows cartoonists to convey more complex ideas than would otherwise be possible. All the cartoons in this section refer to well-known people, but there are cartoons throughout the exhibition that contain references to literature and films.

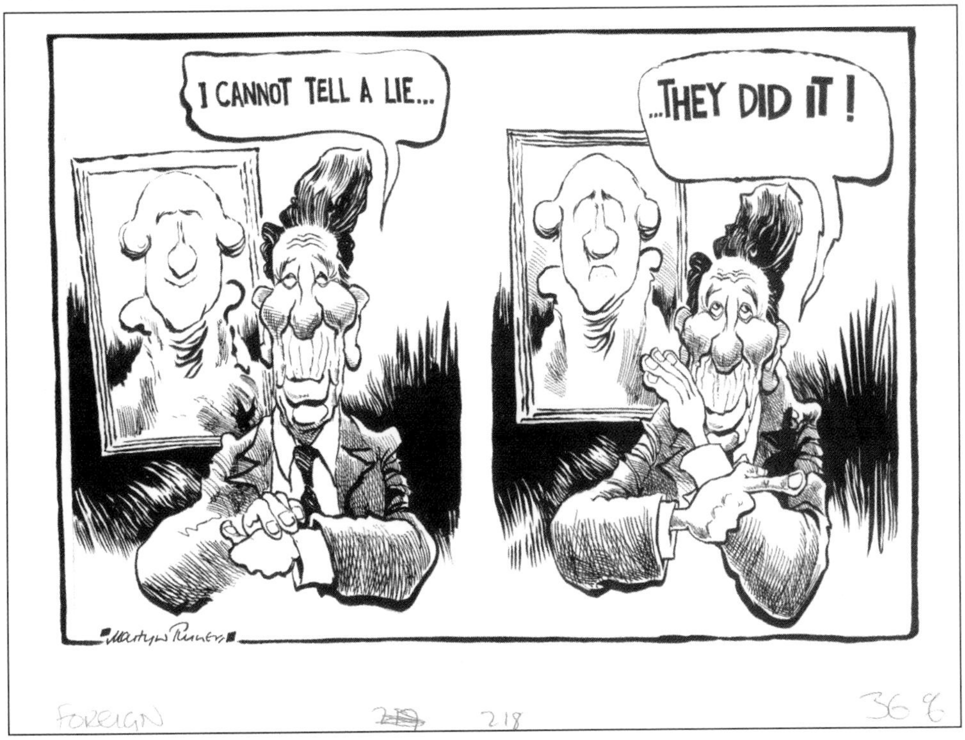
I CANNOT TELL A LIE...
...THEY DID IT!

46) MARTYN TURNER *"I cannot tell a lie..."*

Ink drawing, 25.8 × 27.8 cm. / c. 1980s / Published in the *Irish Times* (Dublin, Ireland)

Cartoonists often criticize contemporary political figures by comparing them to highly regarded leaders of the past and showing them to be wanting. In this cartoon, Turner references a well-known anecdote about President George Washington's childhood invented by Mason Locke Parson Weems[1] in the fifth edition of his popular book *The Life of George Washington* (1806).[2] According to Weems, the young Washington once damaged a cherry tree in his father's garden while playing with a hatchet. When his father asked him whether he knew anything about it, he responded, "I can't tell a lie, Pa; you know I can't tell a lie. I did cut it with my hatchet."[3]

In this cartoon, a portrait of George Washington looks over President Ronald Reagan's shoulder. It seems that Reagan is about to follow Washington's example by admitting that he is responsible for something, but he instead blames someone else.

## 47) DRAPER HILL *"I cannot tell a lie..."*

Ink and Ben-Day overlay* drawing, 27.7 × 32.5 cm. / September 16, 1998 / Published in the *Detroit News* (Detroit, Michigan)

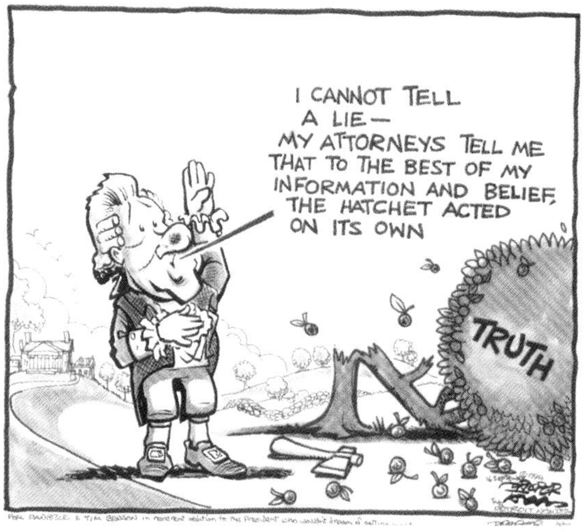
I CANNOT TELL A LIE— MY ATTORNEYS TELL ME THAT TO THE BEST OF MY INFORMATION AND BELIEF THE HATCHET ACTED ON ITS OWN
TRUTH

Like Turner's cartoon (item 46), this cartoon uses Weems's anecdote about the young George Washington and the cherry tree to comment on the dishonesty of a president. In Hill's cartoon, he has depicted President Bill Clinton wearing the clothes and wig usually associated with Washington. Clinton stands over a felled cherry tree labeled "Truth" and a hatchet. However, rather than claiming responsibility for what he has obviously done, Clinton swears on the advice of his attorneys that the hatchet acted on its own. This is a reference to the fact that many felt Clinton used evasive language during the events leading up to his impeachment in 1998.[1]

## 48) ART YOUNG *1860 the rail splitter; 1912 the lion killer*

Ink drawing, 18 × 20.5 cm. / 1912 / Publication status unknown

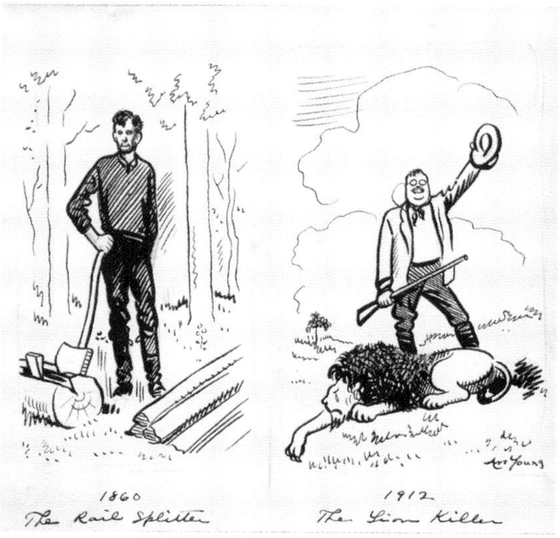
1860
The Rail Splitter
1912
The Lion Killer

Like George Washington, President Abraham Lincoln is frequently used as a yardstick by which cartoonists measure other presidents. In this case, Young compares President Theodore Roosevelt to Lincoln. After serving as president from 1901 to 1909, Roosevelt refused to run for reelection, instead selecting William Howard Taft as his successor. He then went on a year-long safari in Africa on which he killed many animals, including nine lions. Upon his return to the United States, Roosevelt was unhappy with Taft's actions as president, so Roosevelt decided to run for reelection in 1912. When he was unable to get the Republican nomination, he started the Progressive, "Bull Moose Party," ultimately splitting Republican voters and allowing Woodrow Wilson to win the election.[1]

In this cartoon, Young shows Roosevelt as a "lion killer," something he indicates is not admirable by showing a tear sliding down the snout of the dead lion at Roosevelt's feet and showing Roosevelt posing theatrically. By contrast, Young has shown Lincoln as the "Rail Splitter," a reference to the story that Lincoln had worked splitting rails in his youth.[2] In contrast to Roosevelt's self-satisfied posing, Lincoln appears diligent and reserved. Young seems to be suggesting that Roosevelt is more show than substance.

*Ben-Day overlays are transparent sheets covered in evenly-spaced dots that some cartoonists use to create shading effects in their drawings. The artist cuts the shape of the shaded area out of the sheet and attaches it to the drawing.

## 49) ART YOUNG *The Republican Party down to date—*

Ink drawing, 24.5 × 16 cm. / 1924 / Published in Art Young and Heywood Broun's *The Best of Art Young*, New York: Vanguard Press, 1936

Like Young's cartoon of Presidents Abraham Lincoln and Theodore Roosevelt (item 48), this cartoon criticizes a contemporary political figure by comparing him to Lincoln. In this case, Young's target is Calvin Coolidge. Lincoln is depicted as a tall, classical bust, while Coolidge is comically small and dressed in a business suit. This suggests that the leaders of the Republican Party have deteriorated from heroes like Lincoln to unremarkable men like Coolidge.

## 50) CY HUNGERFORD *Indestructible!*

Ink drawing, 41.8 × 31.4 cm. / 1941 / Published in the *Pittsburgh Post-Gazette* (Pittsburgh, Pennsylvania)

In this World War II-era cartoon, Hungerford, like Art Young (item 49), has used an image of a statue of President Lincoln to make his point. However, rather than comparing Lincoln to a political figure of the time, Hungerford has used the statue of Lincoln in the Lincoln Memorial as a symbol for the strength of the United States. Tiny, cartoonish figures of Adolf Hitler, Benito Mussolini, and Emperor Hirohito hit the statue with mallets, but it remains undamaged, suggesting that the Axis powers will not be able to damage the United States, either.

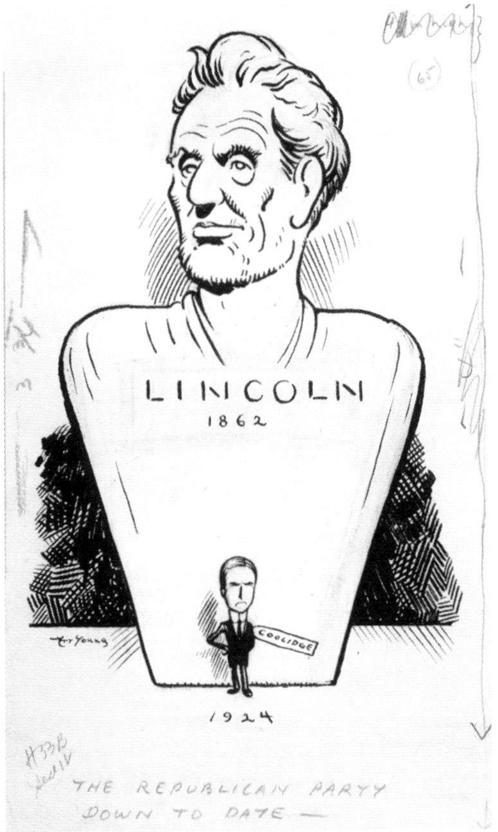
LINCOLN
1862
COOLIDGE
1924
THE REPUBLICAN PARTY
DOWN TO DATE —

ITEM 49

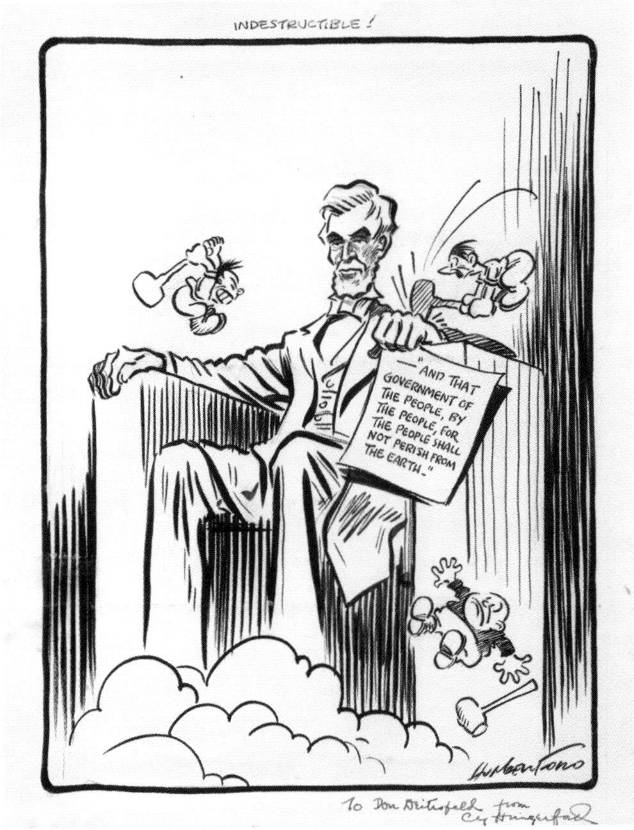
INDESTRUCTIBLE!
—"AND THAT GOVERNMENT OF THE PEOPLE, BY THE PEOPLE, FOR THE PEOPLE SHALL NOT PERISH FROM THE EARTH."

ITEM 50

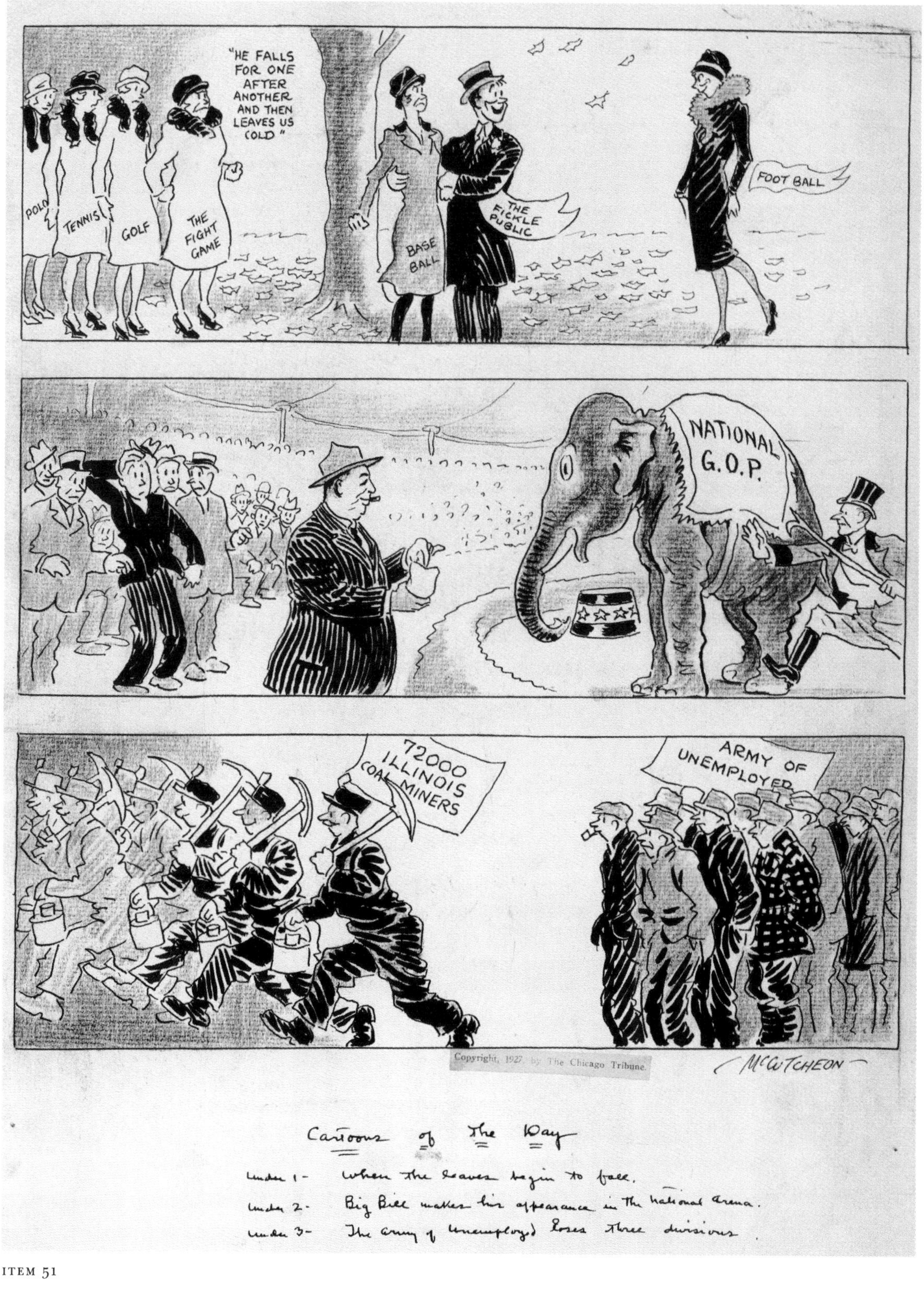
"HE FALLS FOR ONE AFTER ANOTHER AND THEN LEAVES US COLD"
POLO
TENNIS
GOLF
THE FIGHT GAME
BASE BALL
THE FICKLE PUBLIC
FOOT BALL
NATIONAL G.O.P.
72000 ILLINOIS COAL MINERS
ARMY OF UNEMPLOYED
Copyright, 1927, by The Chicago Tribune.
McCUTCHEON

Cartoons of The Day

Under 1- When the leaves begin to fall.

Under 2- Big Bill makes his appearance in the National Arena.

Under 3- The army of unemployed loses three divisions.

ITEM 51

# V ❦ History of the Collection

The items in this section provide an overview of my collecting areas of interest. They include my first political cartoon, an item related to Irish history, and my first Japanese print.

## 51) JOHN T. MCCUTCHEON *Cartoons of the day*

Ink and crayon drawing, 33.5 × 29.3 cm. / October 1927 / Published in the *Chicago Tribune* (Chicago, Illinois)

This is the first political cartoon I acquired for my collection (see description of acquisition in the introduction to this catalog).

The cartoon consists of three panels, each depicting a different subject. The top panel is a gag cartoon about the American public's infatuation with a different sport each season. The bottom panel is a comment on the end of a long strike by 72,000 coal miners in Illinois. The strike began on April 1, 1927, and the mines remained closed until the union representatives and the mine operators reached an agreement on October 2, 1927.[1]

The most interesting panel is the middle one, which depicts Chicago mayor William Hale Thompson, popularly known as "Big Bill" Thompson, tempting an elephant labeled "National GOP" with peanuts. This is a reference to Big Bill Thompson's presidential ambitions. He hoped to become the Republican nominee for president at the Republican National Convention of 1928 and had used his position as Chicago's mayor to amass a sizeable amount of money to support his campaign, but he could not garner enough support from the Illinois delegation to get the nomination.[2] On Thompson's death, his safe-deposit boxes were found to be filled with cash, bonds, and stocks worth over $1.84 million.[3]

## 52) JACK B. YEATS *A Broadside*

No. 1 (New Series), Cuala Press, 29.5 × 21.8 cm. / January 1937 / Eds. Dorothy Wellesley and W. B. Yeats

My collection includes a significant amount of material on and from Ireland, like this broadside.

This broadside was published by Cuala Press, which had its origins in the Dun Emer Arts and Crafts cooperative organized by Evelyn Gleeson. In 1902, Gleeson invited Elizabeth C. "Lolly" Yeats and Susan "Lily" Yeats, the sisters of the famous Irish poet William Butler Yeats, to join the cooperative. Lily Yeats managed Dun Emer's embroidery department and Lolly Yeats managed the printing press. In 1908, Lily and Lolly separated from Dun Emer and founded Cuala Industries, which consisted of an embroidery shop run by Lily and a press run by Lolly. Cuala Press was part of the Celtic Revival or Irish Renaissance, a cultural movement in Ireland that sought to revive Irish cultural heritage.[1]

One of Cuala Press's most successful productions was the series known as *A Broadside*, which sometimes featured poems by their brother William and illustrations by their other brother, Jack Butler Yeats. This series was originally started by Jack B. Yeats under the name *A Broad Sheet* a few years before the founding of Cuala Press. After Lolly Yeats formed Cuala Press, she revived the publication in 1908. The first series ran from 1908 to 1915,[2] the second in 1935, and the third in 1937.[3]

This broadside from the third series features an illustration by Jack B. Yeats and a poem by William Butler Yeats titled "Come Gather Round Me Parnellites" on its cover. This poem was first published

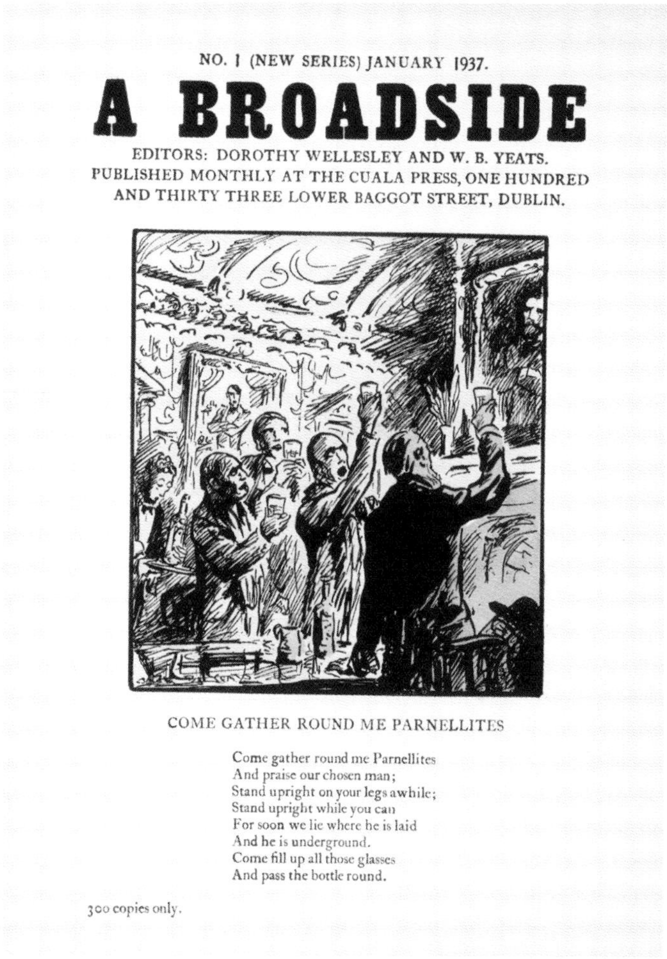
NO. I (NEW SERIES) JANUARY 1937.

A BROADSIDE

EDITORS: DOROTHY WELLESLEY AND W. B. YEATS.
PUBLISHED MONTHLY AT THE CUALA PRESS, ONE HUNDRED AND THIRTY THREE LOWER BAGGOT STREET, DUBLIN.

COME GATHER ROUND ME PARNELLITES

Come gather round me Parnellites
And praise our chosen man;
Stand upright on your legs awhile;
Stand upright while you can
For soon we lie where he is laid
And he is underground.
Come fill up all those glasses
And pass the bottle round.

300 copies only.

in 1937,[4] so this is likely the poem's first appearance in print. In his later years, William Butler Yeats frequently produced works that celebrated Irish Parliamentary Party leader Charles Stewart Parnell, who was a Protestant landowner in Ireland and one of the most influential advocates for Home Rule.[5] Home Rule was a political movement in Ireland that supported self-government for Ireland within the United Kingdom of Great Britain and Ireland, but not complete separation from the United Kingdom.[6] For much of his life, Yeats was a supporter of Home Rule and wary of Republicanism, which advocated for the complete independence of Ireland. However, after the Irish Revolution, Yeats was appointed as a senator in the newly established Senate of the Irish Free State in 1922 and was embraced as a "poet of the revolution."[7]

This is the first stanza of Yeats's "Come Gather Round Me Parnellites" printed on this broadside:

> Come gather round me Parnellites
> And praise our chosen man;
> Stand upright on your legs awhile;
> Stand upright while you can
> For soon we lie where he is laid
> And he is underground.
> Come fill up all those glasses
> And pass the bottle round.

## 53) YOSHITOSHI *Fifteen Tokugawa shoguns*

Triptych color woodblock print, 36 × 75 cm. / 1875

My collection also contains a large number of Japanese prints. This is the first one I acquired. I was browsing Japanese woodblock prints at the Chicago Antiques Show and liked them, but I had no interest in purchasing one until the dealer brought out this item and explained its political context.

The print depicts the fifteen Tokugawa shoguns of Japan. The Tokugawa shogunate was a military regime that controlled Japan from 1603 to 1868. This is also known as the Edo period. While Japan had an emperor during this period, he was primarily symbolic and the real leader of the country was the warrior clans, known as the shogun. Toyotomi Hideyoshi had succeeded in uniting Japan in 1590 after a long period of conflict between the military clans of Japan, and on his death, his military advisor Tokugawa Ieyasu (1543–1616) seized power and declared himself shogun.[1] He is the figure in the center of the print dressed in traditional Japanese armor. Another noteworthy figure is Tokugawa Tsunayoshi (1646–1709), the fifth shogun popularly known as the "Dog Shogun." Tsunayoshi issued a series of infamous laws known as the "Edicts on Compassion for Living Things," which forbade people from harming animals, particularly dogs. In at least one case, a man was executed for striking a dog. When the city of Edo was nearly overrun by stray dogs as a result of this policy, he even built kennels to care for as many as 50,000 dogs at government expense.[2,3] He is the figure seated with a dog in the print.

The power of the Tokugawa shogunate began to falter in the mid-19th century as Japan faced economic difficulties and many of its citizens began pressuring the shogunate to lift its long-standing restrictions on trade and travel between their country and the rest of the world.[4] The fifteenth and final shogun was Tokugawa Yoshinobu. This shogun tried to institute reforms to strengthen the shogunate and reached out to France in an effort to secure its support for his government, but internal divisions prevailed. While some of his advisors and supporters continued to try to preserve the old government, Yoshinobu himself put up little struggle against the Meiji Restoration in 1868,[5] which replaced the shogunate with rule by imperial forces and ushered in a period of intense industrialization and Westernization in Japan.[6] Tokugawa Yoshinobu is the figure seated on a stool wearing Western style dress.

# VI ❦ Art of the Political

The items in this group are examples of works by well-known cartoonists, cartoons about cartoonists and cartooning, and items that illustrate aspects of the art of creating political cartoons.

### 54) JAMES GILLRAY *End of the Irish farce of Catholic Emancipation*

Etching, 39.3 × 46.3 cm. / *The Works of James Gillray*, London: Henry G. Bohn, 1851 / (Original print published in 1805 by Hannah Humphrey of London, England)

James Gillray is sometimes credited with inventing the genre of British political caricature.[1] This cartoon is a good example of how early political cartoons differ from modern ones. Rather than having only a few figures and a simple caption, Gillray's cartoon includes around twenty figures, extensive embedded text, and a lengthy quote from John Milton's *Paradise Lost* as its caption. Whereas most of today's political cartoons are intended to be viewed and understood within a few seconds, Gillray clearly expected his audiences to spend much more time with his cartoons. In fact, people who could not afford to buy their own copies of his cartoons could rent a portfolio of them for an evening's entertainment.[2]

This cartoon is a reference to the introduction of the first Irish petition for Catholic Emancipation in 1805. The petitioners objected to the fact that Irish Catholics were barred from holding certain offices and had no voice in their government.[3] The petition was introduced into the House of Lords by Lord William Grenville (the figure in bishop's robes staggering backwards, his arms flung upward as a scroll labeled "Catholic Petition" is blown from his hands) on May 10, 1805 and into the House of Commons by Charles Fox (the figure seated on the bull, a symbol of Ireland) on May 13, 1805. Gillray refers to the petition as a farce because King George III and many others opposed it, so those introducing the petition knew it had no chance of succeeding.

The cartoon contains many identifiable figures. Among them are the faces of William Pitt the Younger; Robert Jenkinson, second Earl of Liverpool; and Henry Addington, first Viscount Sidmouth blowing back the petitioners. Behind Lord William Grenville, George Grenville, Marquess of Buckingham, is dressed as a monk. Francis Hastings, first Marquess of Hastings and second Earl of Moira, has fallen into a sitting position, his leg flung upwards. Mrs. Fitzherbert, the Catholic mistress of the Prince of Wales (the future George IV), is dressed as an abbess and sprawls below the rearing bull. Most of the other figures are identifiable people, as well, and all these figures would likely have been recognizable to viewers of the time.[4]

This print, originally published in 1805, is from Henry George Bohn's 1851 edition of Gillray's work, which was printed from Gillray's original plates.

## 55) GEORGE WOODWARD (DRAWING); ISAAC CRUIKSHANK (ETCHING) *Billy's fantoccini or John Bull over curious*

ITEM 55A

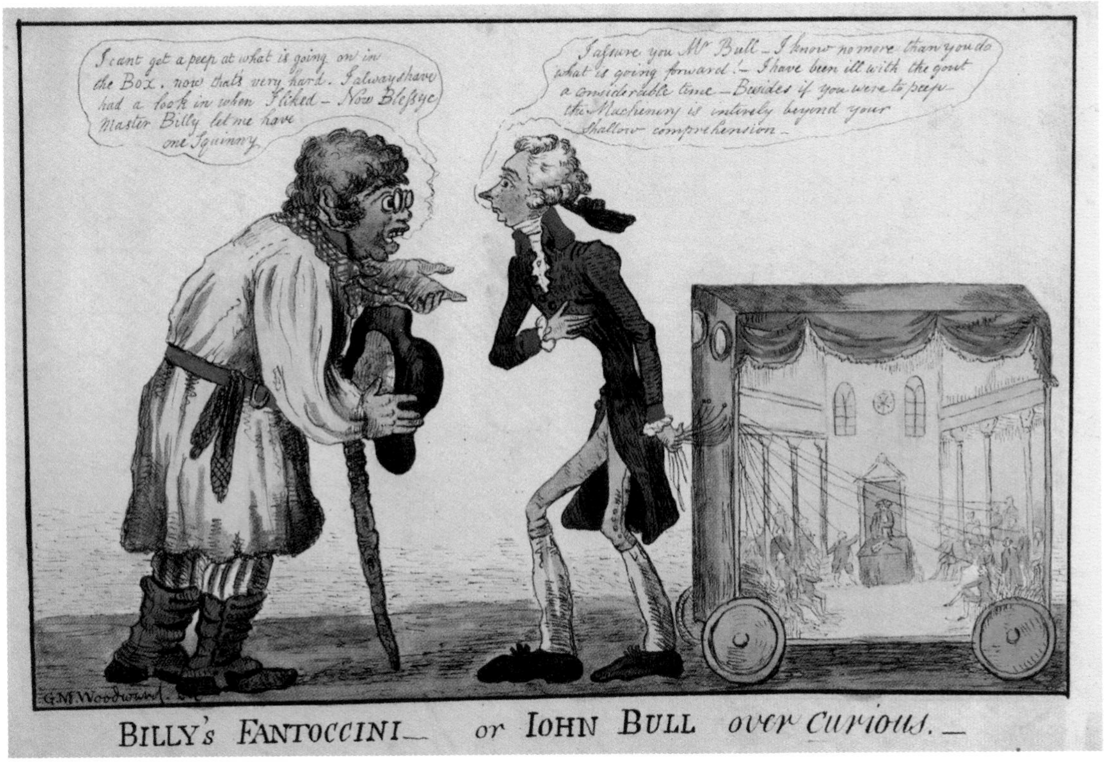
I cant get a peep at what is going on in the Box. now that's very hard. I always have had a look in when I liked – Now Bless ye Master Billy let me have one Squinny.
I assure you Mr Bull – I know no more than you do what is going forward! – I have been ill with the gout a considerable time – Besides if you were to peep – the Machinery is intirely beyond your shallow comprehension –
G.M. Woodward
BILLY's FANTOCCINI – or JOHN BULL over curious. –

ITEM 55B

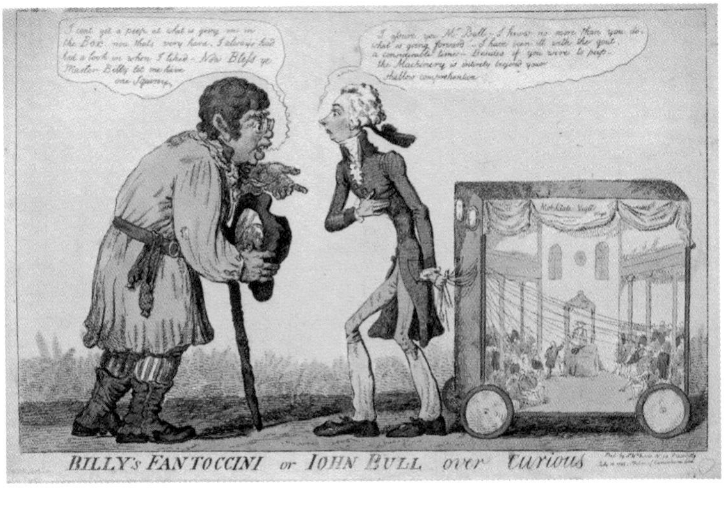
BILLY's FANTOCCINI or JOHN BULL over curious

Ink and watercolor drawing (55a), 26 × 38.5 cm., and hand-colored etching (55b), 25.5 × 39.5 cm., after the drawing by Woodward / July 16, 1798 / Published by S. W. Fores of London, England

This cartoon depicts John Bull, a symbol of the common Englishman, and William Pitt the Younger, who served as prime minister of Great Britain from 1783 to 1801 and from 1804 to 1806.[1] Pitt was the youngest man ever to become prime minister: he was only 24 years old in 1783.[2] In the cartoon, Pitt is towing a fantoccini (a puppet show operated by strings or mechanical devices)[3] of the House of Commons. The galleries are empty, and all the figures inside are puppets to which Pitt holds the strings. John Bull leans forward, trying to see the interior, and says, "I cant get a peep at what is going on in the Box. now thats very hard. I always had had a look in when I liked - Now Bless ye Master Billy let me have one Squiny." Pitt replies, "I assure you Mr Bull—I know no more than you do, what is going forward!—I have been ill with the gout, a considerable time—Besides if you were to peep—the Machinery is intirely beyond your shallow comprehention!"

According to the British Museum, this cartoon is a reference to the clearing of the House of Commons of strangers (visitors who are not members of Parliament or other parliamentary officials) for debates on Ireland on June 14 and 21, 1798.[4]

## 56) LESLIE WARD ("SPY") *Men of the day. No. 185. Mr. John Tenniel.*

Color lithograph, 33.5 × 19.5 cm. / October 26, 1878 / Published in *Vanity Fair* (London, England)

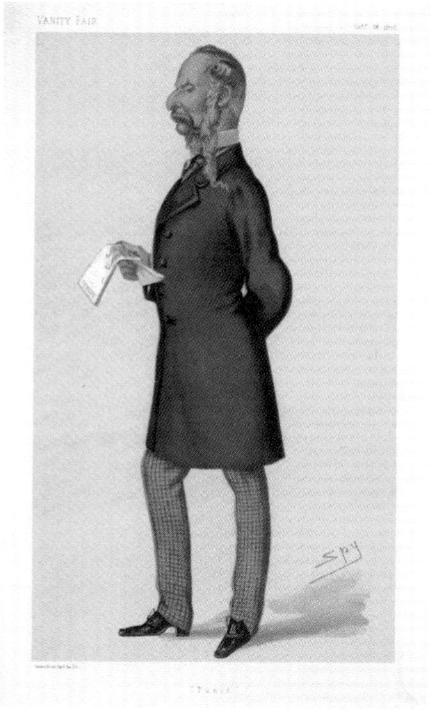
VANITY FAIR

This caricature from *Vanity Fair* depicts Sir John Tenniel, a cartoonist for *Punch* and an illustrator best known for his illustrations for Lewis Carroll's *Alice's Adventures in Wonderland* and *Through the Looking-Glass*. He achieved great professional and social success and recognition, and was knighted by Queen Victoria in 1893.[1] Ward's caricature of Tenniel is not unflattering, and the accompanying text is largely complimentary. Tenniel is an example of a cartoonist who achieved social success and professional recognition, and this cartoon shows him as a successful man at the top of his profession.

## 57) ART YOUNG *The blow that almost killed a cartoonist*

Ink drawing, 17 × 20.5 cm. / c. 1914 / Publication status unknown

In contrast to Ward's complimentary caricature of the successful cartoonist Sir John Tenniel, this self-portrait by Art Young comments on Young's status as an outsider in his profession. In 1914, Young was nominated for membership in the National Press Club, but was rejected. In his autobiography, Young writes that "my record was against me, particularly the cartoon attacking the Associated Press, for which I had been indicted. Some of the membership committee (and especially one who had proposed me) dissented vigorously against the attitude of those to whom I was anathema. But it did no good then." Young also notes that he was "under a cloud" at the time because of a libel suit brought against him by the Associated Press.[1]

Young shows himself ill and tucked into bed, holding a rejection notice from the National Press Club while a cloud of "impenetrable gloom" hangs over his head. A very similar drawing was published in his autobiography, *Art Young, His Life and Times*. This may be a rough sketch for that drawing.

BULLETIN.
ART YOUNG
MAY RECOVER
AFTER BEING SOCIALLY ANNIHILATED BY THE NATIONAL PRESS CLUB, HE REGAINS CONSCIOUSNESS
IMPENETRABLE GLOOM
NOTICE OF REJECTION FROM National Press Club

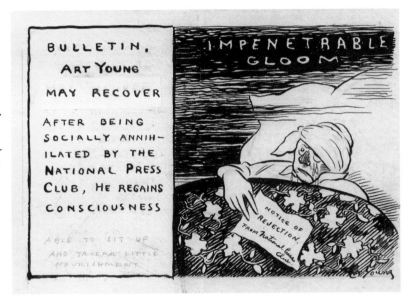

## 58) DOUG MARLETTE *"Pssst! Tell me it ain't Hubert!"*

Wood and metal printing block and print, 8.5 × 10 cm. / c. 1972 / Published by the *Charlotte Observer* (Charlotte, North Carolina)

Hubert H. Humphrey, the Democratic nominee for president in 1968, was seen by some Democratic voters as weak-willed,[1] and some political commentators argued that his running mate, Edmund Muskie, would make a better presidential candidate than either Humphrey or his opponent, Richard M. Nixon.[2]

Humphrey and Muskie lost to Nixon in the 1968 election by one of the smallest margins in history, but this defeat did not bring Humphrey's political ambitions to an end. After a brief stint as a professor of public affairs at the University of Minnesota, Humphrey was reelected to the Senate in 1970 and once again sought the Democratic presidential nomination in 1972.[3] In this cartoon, a donkey (the symbol of the Democratic Party) peers nervously over his shoulder into a mirror labeled "one peek reveals the Democratic presidential nominee for 1972," hoping he will not see Humphrey as the face of the Democratic Party in 1972. Marlette seems to be indicating that some Democrats feared that if Humphrey was nominated he would repeat his performance in 1968 and the party would be defeated.

MARLETTE
Magic Mirror
ONE PEEK REVEALS THE DEMOCRATIC PRESIDENTIAL NOMINEE for 1972
"PSSST! TELL ME IT AIN'T HUBERT!"

Worries that Humphrey would receive the Democratic presidential nomination were not realized, since the nomination went to George McGovern.[4] McGovern, however, lost to

incumbent President Nixon by one of the largest margins in American history,[5] which calls into question whether these doubts about Humphrey's viability as a candidate were warranted.

At one time, political cartoons were usually printed using blocks like these, and this is as an example of such a block and its product.

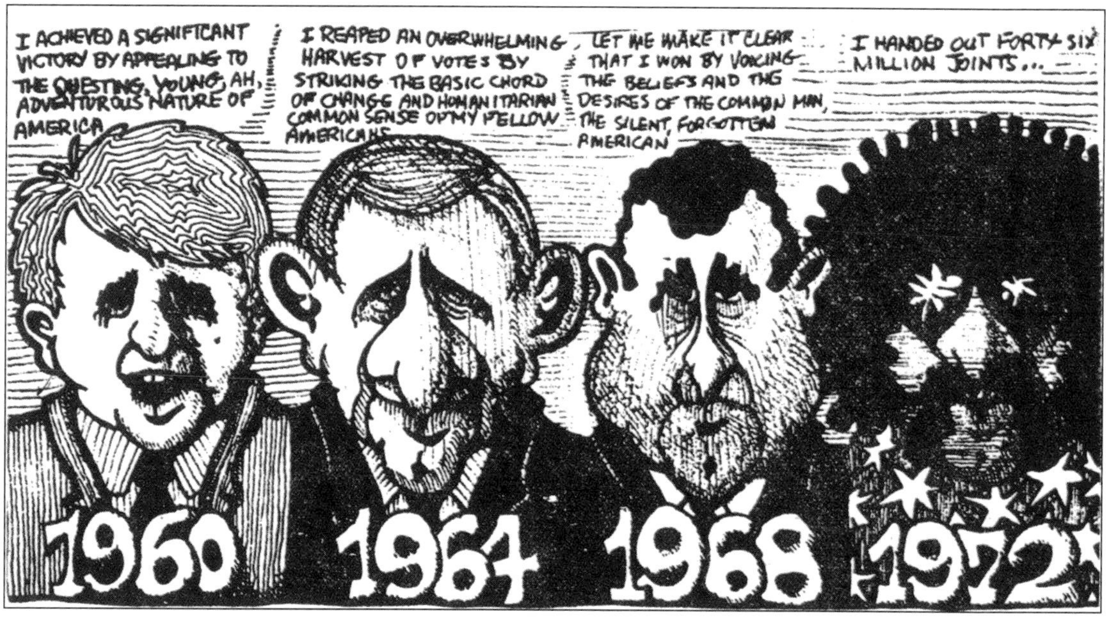
I ACHIEVED A SIGNIFICANT VICTORY BY APPEALING TO THE QUESTING, YOUNG, AH, ADVENTUROUS NATURE OF AMERICA
I REAPED AN OVERWHELMING HARVEST OF VOTES BY STRIKING THE BASIC CHORD OF CHANGE AND HUMANITARIAN COMMON SENSE OF MY FELLOW AMERICANS
LET ME MAKE IT CLEAR THAT I WON BY VOICING THE BELIEFS AND THE DESIRES OF THE COMMON MAN, THE SILENT, FORGOTTEN AMERICAN
I HANDED OUT FORTY-SIX MILLION JOINTS...
1960
1964
1968
1972

## 59) UNKNOWN ARTIST *1960, 1964, 1968, 1972*

Wood and metal print block and print, 7.7 × 15 cm. / c. 1972 / Probably published in a student newspaper

In this cartoon, the unknown artist comments on the cultural shift the United States experienced between 1960 and 1972. This shift, which became visible in the mid-1960s, is often called the "counterculture" movement, and its adherents were usually skeptical of traditional values and advocated for personal freedom. The counterculture was also strongly associated with recreational drug use.[1]

The first figure in this cartoon, President John F. Kennedy (elected in 1960), states "I achieved a significant victory by appealing to the questing, young, ah, adventurous nature of America." The second figure, President Lyndon B. Johnson (elected in 1964), declares "I reaped an overwhelming harvest of votes by striking the basic chord of change and humanitarian common sense of my fellow Americans." The third figure, President Richard M. Nixon (elected in 1968), proclaims "Let me make it clear that I won by voicing the beliefs and the desires of the common man, the silent, forgotten American." The final figure (shown under the year 1972) is not a specific person, but rather a representation of the countercultural movement, and he asserts "I handed out forty-six million joints." According to the person from whom I purchased these blocks, this cartoon was probably published in a student newspaper, so it is difficult to tell whether the artist is making a real criticism of the countercultural movement or teasing it good-naturedly.

This is another example of a printing block with the print it produced.

## 60) RALPH YARDLEY *Autumn gusts*

Ink and pencil drawing and clipping, 27.7 × 23.8 cm. / October 22, 1948 / Published in the *Stockton Record* (Stockton, California)

*Caption:* Autumn gusts / Inconsistency of President has emphasized divisions within Democratic Party.

In the weeks leading up to the 1948 presidential election, most political analysts and polls predicted that Democrat Harry S. Truman, who had assumed the presidency upon Franklin D. Roosevelt's death on April 12, 1945, would lose to his Republican challenger, Thomas E. Dewey.[1] This cartoon by Ralph Yardley reflects that popular opinion, showing President Truman frantically trying to gather all the leaves in his yard into a pile labeled "Democratic Party" while the wind blows them over the fence and onto a pile in Dewey's yard labeled "GOP." Like many others, Yardley seems to have believed that Dewey's victory was inevitable.

Truman, however, would ultimately win the election. His victory surprised many, a fact memorialized by the famous photograph of a smiling Truman holding a November 3, 1948 issue of the *Chicago Tribune* with the headline "Dewey Defeats Truman."[2]

The original drawing of this cartoon is accompanied by a clipping of the cartoon as it was printed in the *Stockton Record*. This shows how the level of detail in the original drawings created by cartoonists compares to the printed version most people see.

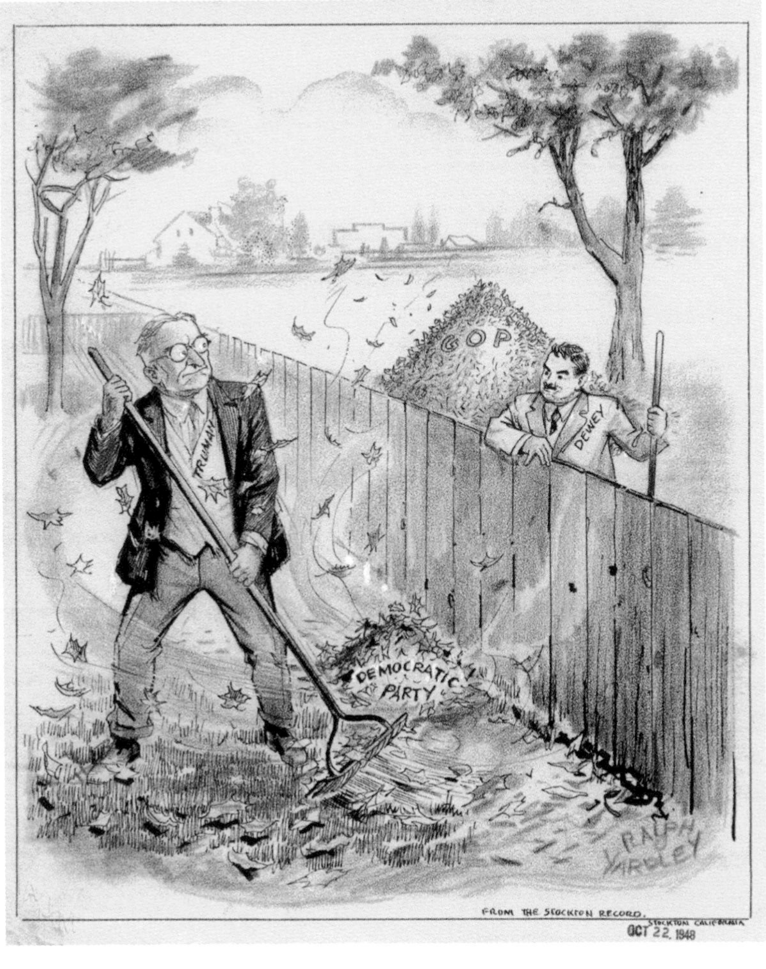
GOP
TRUMAN
DEWEY
DEMOCRATIC PARTY
RALPH YARDLEY
FROM THE STOCKTON RECORD,
STOCKTON CALIFORNIA
OCT 22 1948

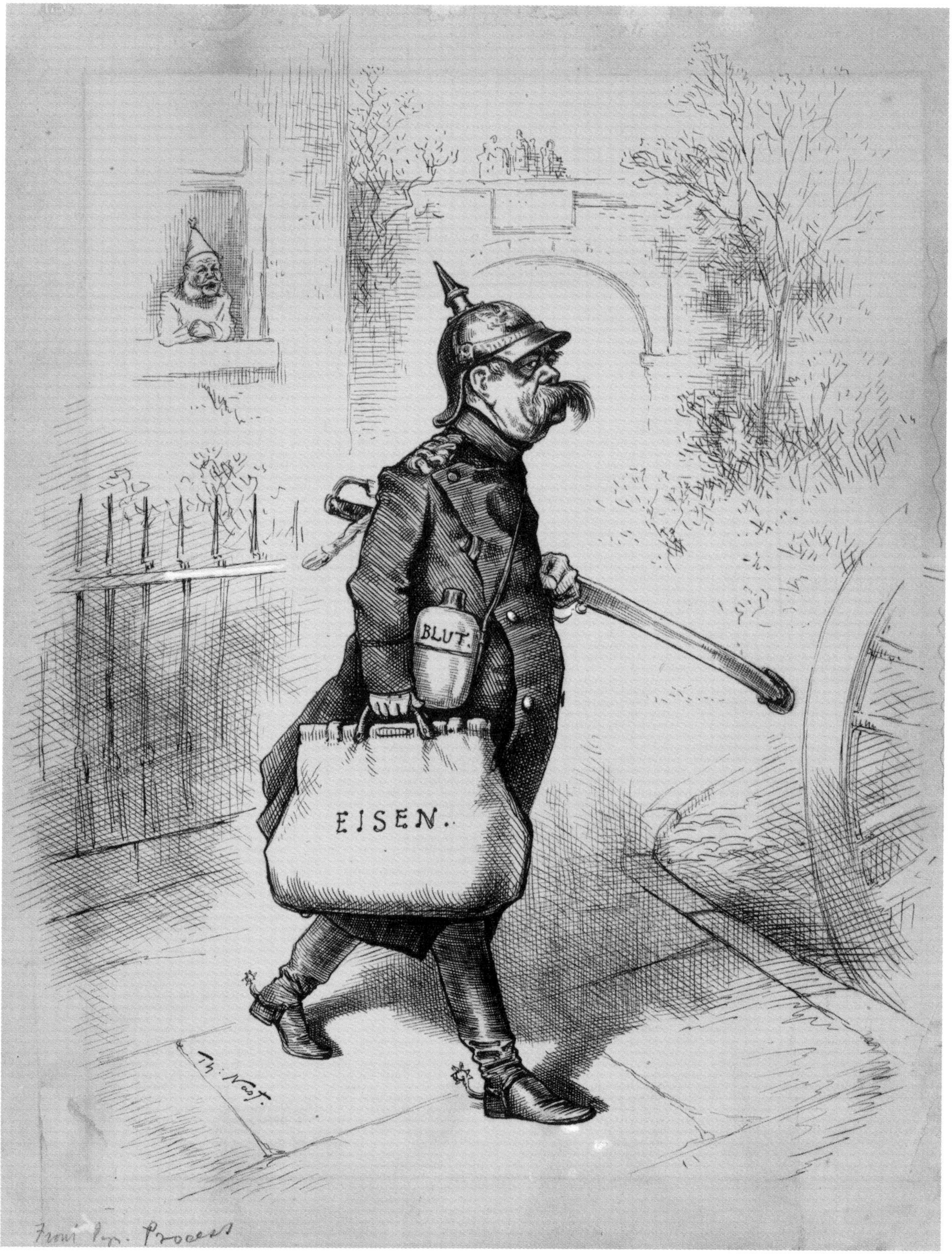
BLUT.
EISEN..
Th: Nast.

ITEM 61

# VII ❧ Highlights and Miscellaneous

The items in this section are highlights from my collections. Some of them tie into the themes of the exhibition, while others are simply interesting.

## 61) THOMAS NAST *Chancellor Bismarck "Coming to America"*

Ink drawing, 35 × 29.5 cm. / June 26, 1880 / Published in *Harper's Weekly* (New York City)

*Caption:* Chancellor Bismarck "Coming to America." Bismarck has resigned again, because he cannot have his own way in his own country. He is coming to America, where each one constitutes a 'one-man power,' and never fails to have his own way.

This drawing by famous American cartoonist Thomas Nast was published on the cover of *Harper's Weekly*. Nast is often considered the first great American cartoonist[1] and is sometimes called the Father of American Caricature.[2] This cartoon depicts Chancellor Otto von Bismarck, the statesman who unified the German states into the German Empire.[3]

On April 6, 1880, the German Bundesrath (Federal Council) voted on a bill that would have required stamps on receipts for postal money orders, which Bismarck supported. The bill was defeated, with 30 votes against it and 28 votes for it. The 30 votes against it represented about 7,500,000 people in the German Empire, while the 28 votes for it represented over 30,000,000 people. After the vote, Bismarck submitted a request to Emperor Wilhelm to be relieved of his duties as chancellor, saying that he could not act on the resolution when it actually represented the will of a minority rather than the majority. The emperor refused to accept his resignation, reportedly replying "Never."[4]

Bismarck ultimately remained chancellor for another decade, until he came into conflict with the young Emperor Wilhelm II, the grandson of the first Wilhelm. Wilhelm II forced Bismarck to resign on March 18, 1890.[5]

In Nast's cartoon, Bismarck strides down a street while Emperor Wilhelm calls to him from a window. Bismarck carries a canteen labeled "Blut" [Blood] and a valise labeled "Eisen" [Iron], a reference to his famous "Blood and Iron" speech in September 1862, when he argued that force would be more successful in unifying Germany than diplomacy.[6]

## 62) SIR JOHN TENNIEL *Little Germanic Magnate*

Ink drawing, 22 × 17 cm. / November 28, 1891 / Published in *Punch* (London, England)

This cartoon by Sir John Tenniel, a successful British cartoonist and illustrator, depicts Emperor Wilhelm II, former German Chancellor Otto von Bismarck, and a figure wearing a sash labeled "socialism" standing before a curtain that reads "Suprema lex regis voluntas" (The king's will is the highest law).[1] Wilhelm holds his scepter, a symbol of his royal power, and the figure representing socialism has reached out to grasp it. Bismarck is shunted off to the side, unable to share the power held by Wilhelm and socialism.

In 1890, Wilhelm II had forced Chancellor Otto von Bismarck, the statesman who is often credited with uniting the German states into a single German Empire,[2] to resign from his position. This conflict was largely due to the fact that Wilhelm did not want to share power with Bismarck,[3] but the split was precipitated by their disagreement over the best way to respond to the growing socialist movement in

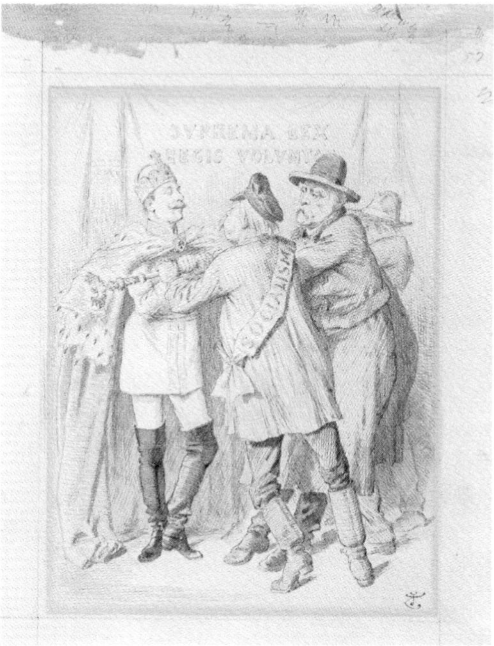
SOCIALISM

Germany. Bismarck wanted to renew laws against socialism despite the resistance of many members of the Reichstag, while Wilhelm thought the best course of action to keep socialism from gaining too much power was to make concessions to the socialists. Additionally, Wilhelm wanted to be popular among his subjects[4] and tried to portray himself as a friend of the working classes.[5] In March of 1890, for instance, Wilhelm had organized the International Labor Conference in Germany.[6] While Bismarck continued to try to influence German politics from time to time, he would never again hold the kind of power he did during his time as chancellor.[7]

Unfortunately for Wilhelm, his efforts did not bring him the popularity he desired, and he ended up resenting the growing power of the Marxist Social Democratic Party.[8]

## 63) E. CUSACHS *"Cab, Guv'nor?"*

Ink drawing, 16 × 30.3 cm. / 1892 / Published in *Boston Evening Transcript* (Boston, Massachusetts)

This cartoon comments on the 1892 election, in which Grover Cleveland was the Democratic nominee for president. Cleveland had served one term as president from 1885 to 1889, but he lost the 1888 election to Republican Benjamin Harrison. Many Americans were unhappy with the administration's

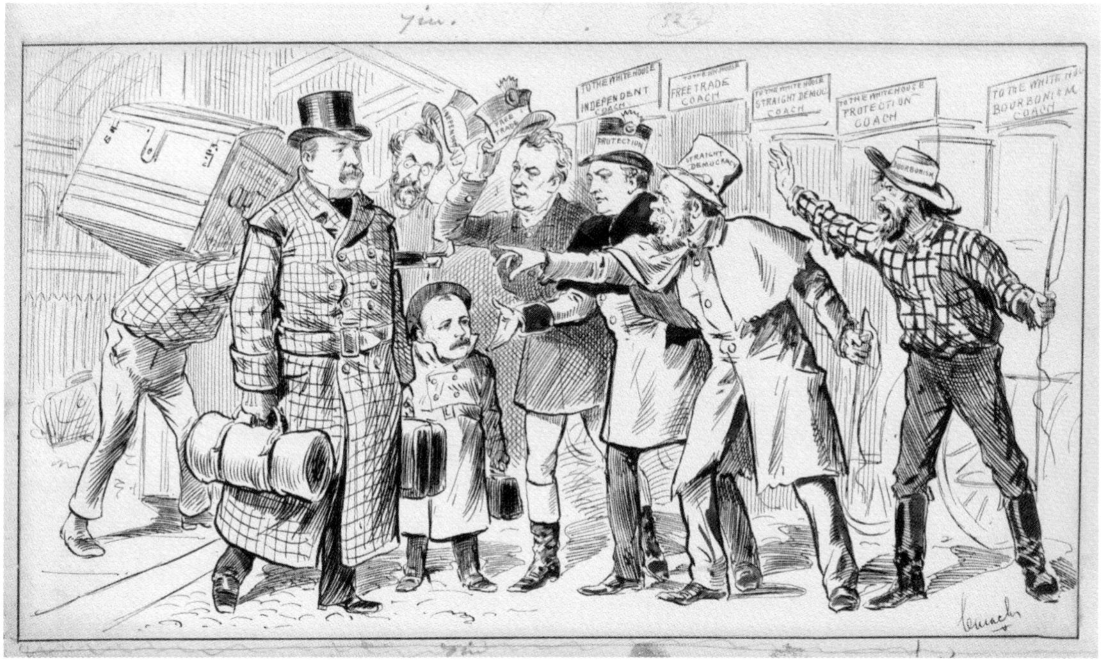
FREE TRADE COACH
PROTECTION

financial policies during the first half of Harrison's term, and in the 1890 elections, the Democrats took control of the House of Representatives and made significant gains in the Senate. There were major divisions in the Democratic Party in 1892, particularly relating to the tariff and of the free coinage of silver. Despite these divisions, the Democratic national convention nominated Cleveland as candidate for president on its first ballot with Adlai Stevenson I as his running mate.[1] Stevenson is the short figure depicted alongside Cleveland. Stevenson's grandson, Adlai Stevenson II, would twice be the Democratic candidate for president and later serve as ambassador to the United Nations.[2] His great-grandson, Adlai Stevenson III, served as a U.S. senator from Illinois.[3] Cleveland and Stevenson won a decisive victory over Harrison in the 1892 election.

In Cusachs's cartoon, several cabs representing different factions of the Democratic Party offer to take Cleveland to the White House, reflecting the eagerness of the Democrats to support Cleveland again. Cusach identifies these factions as those who support free trade, those who support protectionism, straight Democrats, and Bourbon Democrats. The straight Democrats are represented by a figure with ape-like facial features and a clay pipe in his hatband, indicating that he is intended to be an Irish-American[4] (who were strongly associated with the Democratic Party at this time).[5] Another coach represents Independents.

When Cleveland won the 1884 election, he became the first Democratic president since the Civil War. When he won the 1892 election, he became the first and only president to serve two nonconsecutive terms.[6]

## 64) W. CARSON *They don't see me!*

Ink drawing, 30.5 × 30.5 cm. / 1924 / Published in *Akron Beacon News* (Akron, Ohio)

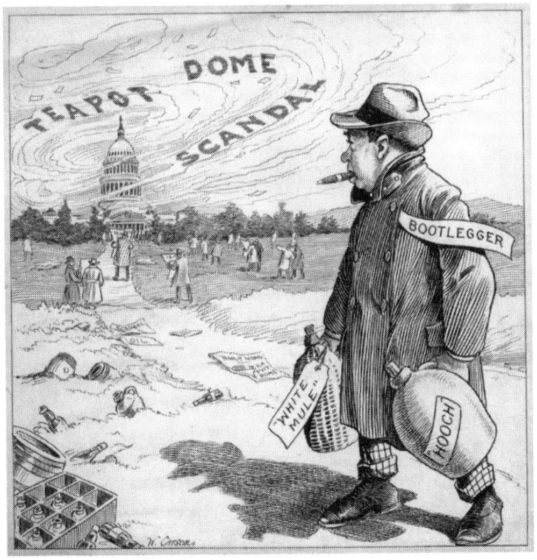
TEAPOT DOME SCANDAL
BOOTLEGGER
WHITE MULE
HOOCH

This cartoon contains references to two things frequently associated with the 1920s—the Teapot Dome Scandal and Prohibition and its circumvention.

News of the Teapot Dome Scandal broke in 1924, but the events of the scandal actually began in 1921. President William Howard Taft had created two oil reserves for the Navy, and in 1915, President Woodrow Wilson created another reserve at Teapot Dome in Wyoming. In 1921, Secretary of the Interior Albert B. Fall convinced President Warren G. Harding to transfer the reserves from the jurisdiction of the Navy to the Department of the Interior.[1] Fall accepted bribes from oil companies and leased the naval reserves to them, including the one at Teapot Dome.[2] Other prominent government officials also became involved in the underhanded dealings. When a Senate investigation led by Montana senator Thomas J. Walsh made the scandal public, it created a media sensation that dominated headlines for months.[3]

In this cartoon, Carson seems to be suggesting that this high-level government corruption was drawing the attention of the public and the media away from an ongoing problem of the time—that of bootleggers who circumvented the ban on alcohol instituted by the Eighteenth Amendment in 1919. Ironically, Prohibition had led to an increase in organized crime as criminals sought to meet the American public's continued demand for alcohol.[4]

## 65) THOMAS NAST *20 years a civil service reformer for himself*

Ink drawing, 20.5 × 20.5 cm. / c. 1876-1884 / Published in *Harper's Weekly* (New York City)

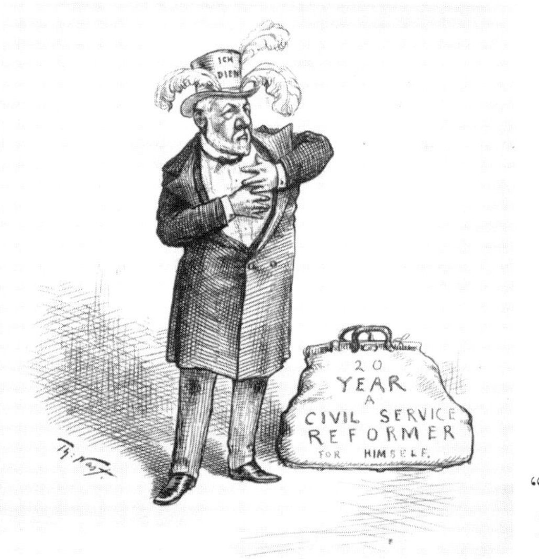
20
YEAR
A
CIVIL SERVICE
REFORMER
FOR HIMSELF.
Th. Nast

This cartoon depicts James G. Blaine, a representative from Maine from 1863 to 1876, Speaker of the House from 1869 to 1874, and a U.S. senator for Maine from 1876 to 1881. He also served as secretary of state in 1881 and from 1889 to 1892. Blaine sought the Republican nomination for president in 1876 and 1880, without success. He finally obtained the nomination in 1884, but was defeated by Democrat Grover Cleveland.[1]

This cartoon refers to Robert Ingersoll's famous speech on June 15, 1876 at the Republican National Convention nominating Blaine for the presidency. In this speech, he praised Blaine extravagantly, saying, "Like an armed warrior, like a plumed knight, James G. Blaine marched down the halls of the American Congress and threw his shining lances full and fair against the brazen foreheads of every defamer of his country and maligner of its honor."[2] While Ingersoll undoubtedly meant his comments sincerely, cartoonist Thomas Nast repeatedly used the sobriquet "The Plumed Knight" to mock Blaine in cartoons like this one.[3] The text on Blaine's bag, "20 year[s] a civil service reformer for himself," is a reference to the rumors of corruption surrounding Blaine. These rumors led to another nickname often associated with Blaine: "Blaine, Blaine, James G. Blaine, continental liar from the state of Maine."[4]

## 66) THOMAS NAST *No upright judge would "uphold the hands of justice" like this!*

Ink drawing, 28 × 20.2 cm. / 1889 / Probably published in *Illustrated American* (Chicago, Illinois)

In this cartoon, Nast criticizes the outcome of the trial of the men accused of murdering Dr. Patrick Henry Cronin of Chicago. Cronin was a member of Clan-na-Gael, a U.S.-based organization headquartered in Chicago that supported Irish independence from Great Britain. The leaders of Clan-na-Gael, Alexander Sullivan, Michael Boland, and D.S. Freely, were known as the "Triangle." Cronin came into conflict with the Triangle when he accused them of misappropriating the organization's funds.

Clan-na-Gael supplied funds to groups in Ireland that shared their goals, and some of its less radical members worried that it was giving money to those involved in the "Fenian Dynamite Campaign."[1,2] This was a bombing campaign waged by Fenians, Irish-Americans who supported the independence of Ireland from Great Britain, in London between 1881 and 1885. It was an early terrorist campaign—the Fenians placed their bombs in highly-trafficked areas and sought to instill fear in the British people so that they would pressure their leaders to grant Ireland independence. The campaign deeply divided Irish-Americans who supported Irish independence, since many did not support the tactics of the Fenian Dynamite Campaign.[3] While the Triangle denied that they had supplied any funds for the campaign, members of Clan-na-Gael, including Cronin, demanded accounts of how all the organization's funds had been spent. Between $100,000 and $250,000 were unaccounted for, suggesting that the members of the Triangle might have embezzled those funds. Cronin continued to press the issue.

The Triangle ultimately accused Cronin of being a traitor and expelled him from the society, which caused a split in the order when thousands of members resigned in solidarity with Cronin. Realizing that they would make no progress towards Irish independence if they didn't coordinate their efforts, the leaders of the various factions eventually came together to try to reunite the organization. They formed a committee, which included Cronin, in 1888 to investigate the actions of the Triangle. When the committee concluded in its final vote that the charges against the Triangle had not been proven, Cronin threatened to make his notes from the trial public. One member of the Triangle, Alexander Sullivan, reportedly said he wanted Cronin "removed."

On May 4, 1889, a man came to Cronin's office and asked that the doctor come with him to assist the man's injured colleague. Cronin and the man left in a carriage together. Cronin did not return that night, and his body was found in a sewer on May 22. Ultimately, five men were brought to trial for Cronin's murder. The prosecution claimed that they were members of a conspiracy organized by the leadership of Clan-na-Gael to assassinate Cronin. One of them was acquitted, one was found guilty of manslaughter, and three were found guilty of first degree murder. Alexander Sullivan, who probably ordered Cronin's murder, was arrested, but the charges against him were dropped due to lack of evidence.[4,5]

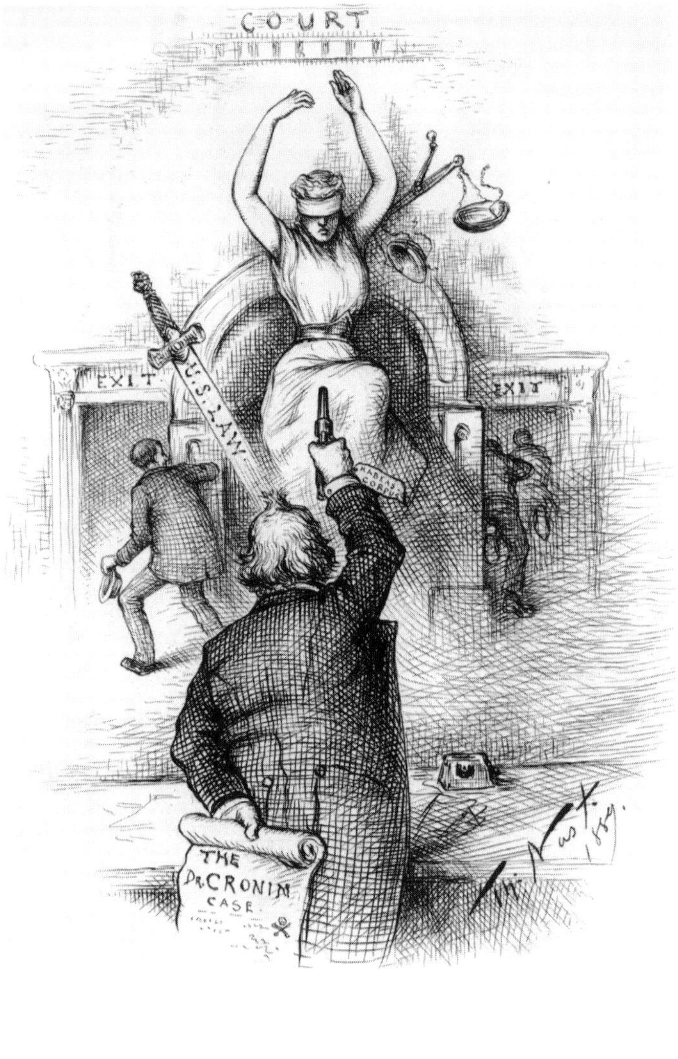
COURT
EXIT
EXIT
U.S. LAW
THE Dr. CRONIN CASE

In this cartoon, Nast criticizes the events surrounding the trial. Since the gun with which Justice is held up is labeled "habeas corpus," he is probably commenting on the fact that Sullivan was released due to lack of evidence. Clan-na-Gael members held many influential positions in Chicago, and, as the convictions in Cronin's trial reveal, were not above using underhanded means to achieve their ends. In fact, several people, including two bailiffs, tried to bribe some of the members of the jury to find in favor of the defendants.[6] Nast clearly thought corruption played a role in the dropping of the charges against Sullivan.

More than a hundred years after this cartoon was published, the issue of Americans' attitudes towards and involvement in the conflict between Ireland and Great Britain continued to resonate (see item 28).

## 67) ARTHUR YOUNG *"Go gettem!"*

Ink and crayon, 27.3 × 43 cm. / c. 1928 / Publication status unknown

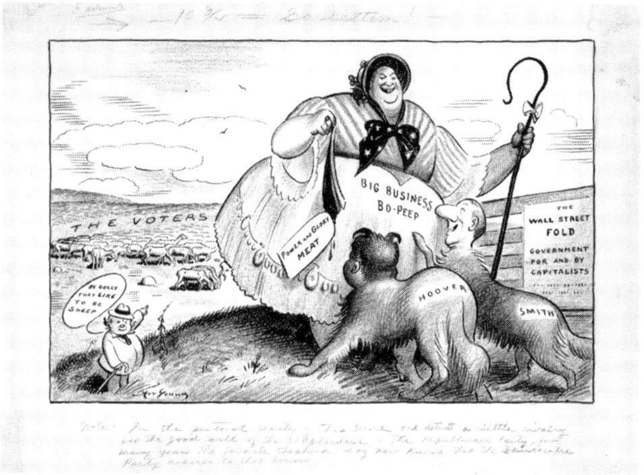
BIG BUSINESS BO-PEEP
THE WALL STREET FOLD
GOVERNMENT FOR AND BY CAPITALISTS
THE VOTERS
HOOVER
SMITH

This cartoon refers to the 1928 presidential election. Herbert Hoover was the Republican candidate, while Al Smith was the Democratic nominee.[1] Hoover had the benefit of campaigning at a time when the U.S. economy had been thriving under a Republican administration. Smith was handicapped by the fact that he was the first Roman Catholic nominated for president by a major U.S. party, and the campaign prompted an outbreak of anti-Catholic sentiment.[2]

However, despite the significant differences between the candidates, Young points out their similarities in this cartoon. Young was a socialist,[3] so he would not have supported either candidate. He depicts both Hoover and Smith as dogs groveling before a figure that represents big business in America. The figure is dressed as a shepherdess while the voters are a flock of sheep in the background. Young has drawn himself in the lower left corner of the drawing saying, "By golly, they like to be sheep." Young seems to see American voters as weak-willed or complacent, their lives completely controlled by powerful businessmen. In his view, political leaders are like sheepdogs—it may seem to the sheep that the dogs are the ones with the power, but the dogs simply do the bidding of the shepherdess.

## 68) KENNETH MAHOOD *The Phoenix*

Ink, gouache, and watercolor drawing, 38 × 35.5 cm. / 1969 / Published in *Punch* (London, England)

The Prague Spring, a brief period of democratic reform in communist-ruled Czechoslovakia, began in January 1968, when Alexander Dubček replaced Antonín Novotný as leader of the Communist Party of Czechoslovakia. The momentum of the movement was slowed when Warsaw Pact and Soviet forces invaded and occupied the country during the night of August 20 to 21, 1968.[1]

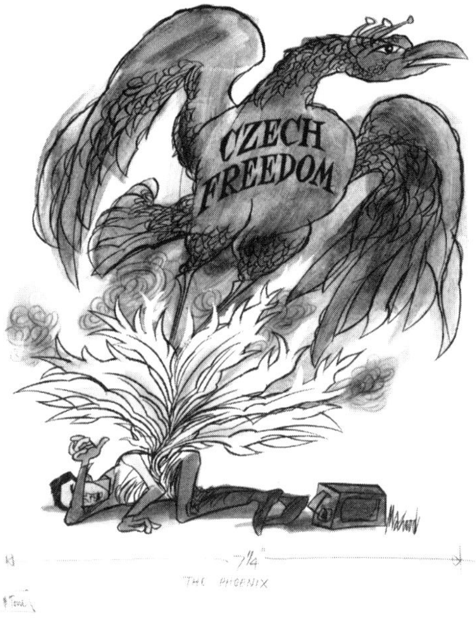
CZECH FREEDOM
THE PHOENIX

On January 16, 1969, Czech student Jan Palach went to Wenceslas Square in the center of Prague, doused himself in gasoline, and set himself on fire to protest the Soviet occupation. He died from his injuries three days later. Palach had hoped his act would galvanize his fellow Czechs and Slovaks to take action to resist the occupying Soviet forces and the return of communist rule. While many attended his funeral, his gesture did not bring about the massive resistance for which he had hoped.[2] Dubček was forced to resign in April 1969 and rigid communist rule was reestablished. Czech freedom would have to wait for another twenty years, when the Velvet Revolution that began in November 1989 brought an end to communist rule in that country.[3]

This dramatic cartoon depicts Palach's self-immolation shortly after the event. The flames rising from his body form a phoenix labeled "Czech freedom," representing his unrealized hopes that his self-sacrifice would help bring freedom to his country.

## 69) KENNETH MAHOOD *Miss Czech Freedom*

Ink, crayon, and watercolor drawing, 46 × 37 cm. 1969 / Published in *Punch* (London, England)

This is another cartoon by Mahood dealing with the Prague Spring and its end, but this drawing has a very different tone than the one of Jan Palach. Here, Mahood has used a naked woman rather than a phoenix to represent Czech freedom. A Soviet soldier with the face of Leonid Brezhnev, leader of the Soviet Communist Party from 1964 to 1982,[1] wearing a hat reading "USSR Decency League" has gagged her.

MISS CZECH FREEDOM
USSR DECENCY LEAGUE

## 70) ART YOUNG *The man who opposes the sale of dope*

Ink drawing, 26 × 22.3 cm. / Unknown date / Publication status unknown

This cartoon depicts William Randolph Hearst, a powerful publisher who, at the peak of his success, owned sixteen newspapers.[1] The reporting in Hearst's newspapers was often sensationalistic, spurred in part by his competition with fellow publisher Joseph Pulitzer. This style of reporting was eventually termed "yellow journalism," and it had a profound influence on the style of journalism in the United States.[2]

In this cartoon, Young criticizes Hearst's style of journalism. Hearst's newspapers launched the famous "reefer madness" campaign about the dangers of marijuana,[3] and Young has taken the opportunity to liken Hearst to a peddler of a different kind of drug. A sign next to Hearst advertises "escape truth and reality... hypocrisy and sophistry for every occasion... Editorials to produce paralysis of thought," and a smaller sign offers "Venom and hatred to kill labor unions." Hearst was virulently anti-union,[4] and Young is clearly suggesting that his publications were biased against unions and used poor reporting techniques.

DOPE JOURNALISM
ESCAPE TRUTH AND REALITY
Ask for My Latest Mixtures...
HYPOCRISY and SOPHISTRY for every occasion.
THIRTY YEARS EXPERIENCE.
EDITORIALS TO PRODUCE PARALYSIS OF THOUGHT.
DOPED NEWS
VENOM AND HATRED TO KILL LABOR UNIONS — ENDORSED — BY BIG INDUSTRIES
PRESCRIPTION DEPARTMENT
HEARST
7" wide

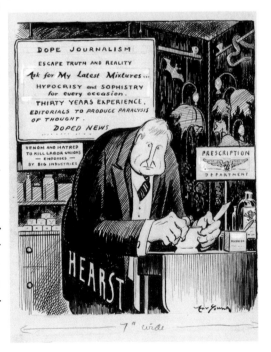

## 71) SIR BERNARD PARTRIDGE *The counter blow*

Ink drawing, 32.7 × 23.5 cm. / April 24, 1940 / Published in *Punch* (London, England)

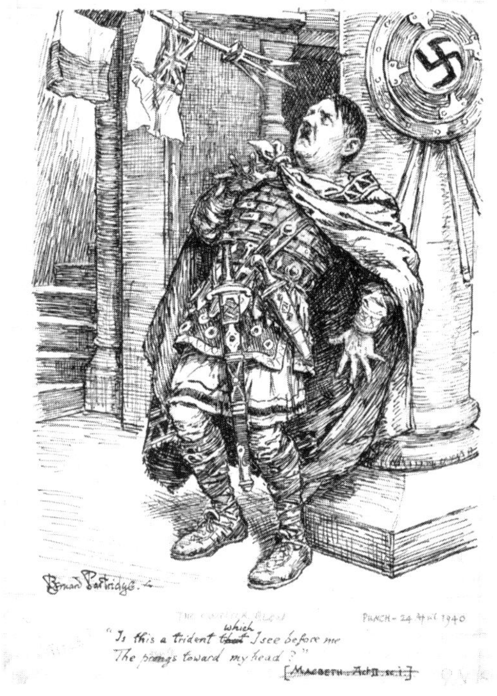
Bernard Partridge.
PUNCH – 24 April 1940
"Is this a trident which I see before me
The prongs toward my head?"
[MACBETH. Act II sc. i.]

*Caption:* The Counter Blow / "Is this a trident which I see before me / the points toward my head?"

This is a cartoon depicting the Allies of World War II cornering Adolf Hitler. The trident bears two flags: the White Ensign of the Royal Navy and the flag of France. The war had begun less than a year before, but it seems the cartoonist sought to show Hitler already on the run; unfortunately, this was overly optimistic. France would fall to Germany by the end of 1940, and the conflict would continue for another five years.[1]

This item is also interesting because it contains a literary reference. The caption echoes two lines from Macbeth's famous soliloquy in Act II, scene one of Shakespeare's *Macbeth*: "Is this a dagger which I see before me, / The handle toward my hand?"[2] The notes below the cartoon show that Partridge originally included the name of the play as part of the caption, but that he crossed it out. This suggests that he expected his audience to understand the reference without assistance.

## 72) HERBERT BLOCK ("HERBLOCK") *London*

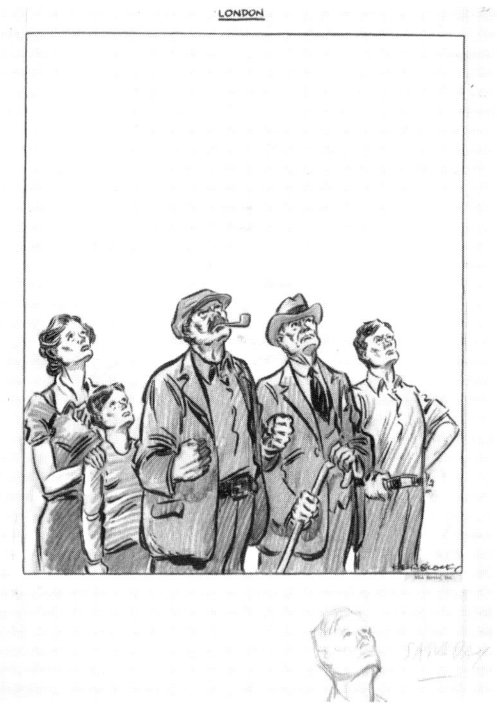
LONDON

Ink and crayon drawing, 46.3 × 32.3 cm. / 1942 / Published by the Newspaper Enterprise Association

This cartoon is a reference to the London Blitz, the protracted bombing campaign by Nazi Germany's Luftwaffe against British civilian targets. Germany's military leaders believed the attack would demoralize the British population, disrupt the British economy, and leave the country vulnerable to invasion. The bombings began on September 7, 1940 and didn't end until May 11, 1941. Even though more than 20,000 British civilians were killed in the air raids and many buildings in London were damaged, the attacks seemed to strengthen British resolve rather than weaken it.[1] The bombings also had the unintended effect of generating sympathy among Americans for the British. Up until the Blitz, the American people largely saw the war as a European conflict and American leaders favored isolationist policies. As reporters published and broadcast harrowing accounts of the bombings, however, the

American people began to admire the resolve of the British and became less detached from the conflict. Additionally, the United States first supplied arms to Britain in response to the Blitz.[2]

This cartoon is a good example of both the changing attitude of Americans towards the war and the kind of publications that were causing that attitude to change. The empty sky that fills most of the frame is ominous, and the figures all look upwards with some trepidation, but their faces reflect more determination than fear. They stand firmly, with no sign of panic. Herblock was an American cartoonist, and this work shows how many Americans viewed the Londoners' endurance.

## 73) JOHN CHASE *Buck Truman rides again*

Ink and watercolor drawing, 40.3 × 30 cm. / November 9, 1948 / Published in *The States* (New Orleans, Louisiana)

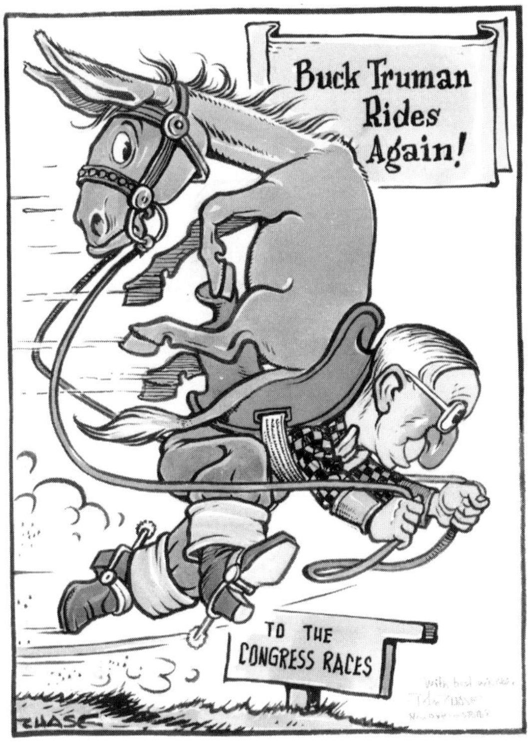
Buck Truman Rides Again!
TO THE CONGRESS RACES
CHASE

Vice President Harry S. Truman had assumed the presidency upon Franklin D. Roosevelt's death on April 12, 1945. As the 1948 presidential election approached, many political analysts and polls predicted that he would lose to the Republican candidate, Thomas E. Dewey.[1] Truman's popularity had been inconsistent during his term, ranging from 87 percent in 1945 to 32 percent in September of 1946. In the November 1946 Congressional elections, Republicans had gained control of both houses of Congress, and most expected that they would take control of the White House in 1948, as well.[2] Truman was also hampered by factions within his party. The most liberal Democrats opposed Truman's Cold War policies and broke off from the party to support Henry A. Wallace's Progressive Party ticket. The Southern Democrats, frequently known as "Dixiecrats," opposed the Democratic Party's moderate support of civil rights and broke off to form the "States Rights Democrats" party with Strom Thurmond as its presidential candidate.[3] All these factors combined to make Dewey seem unbeatable in the 1948 election.

Truman surprised almost everyone by defeating Dewey in the election and going on to a second term.[4] Additionally, the Democrats regained control of both houses in another surprise victory.[5]

In this cartoon, Chase shows Truman running towards "the Congress races" carrying a donkey, symbol of the Democratic Party, on his back. Chase seems to be suggesting that Truman, who had campaigned well,[6] carried the Democratic Party to victory.

## 74) FRANK INTERLANDI *"What am I saying?"*

Ink drawing, 21 × 18 cm. / December 1968 / Published in the *Los Angeles Times* (Los Angeles, California)

BELOW OLYMPUS By Interlandi

GET IN THERE
AND SAVE
THOSE CZECH
COMMUNISTS

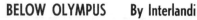

"What am I saying?"

In this small cartoon, Interlandi comments on the reaction of the American public to the invasion of Czechoslovakia by the Soviet army. The Soviets had invaded to end a liberalization movement in Czechoslovakia known as the Prague Spring.[1] In general, the media and the American public reacted to the invasion with sympathy for the Czechs and Slovaks, and many newspaper articles and editorials expressed displeasure with the lack of response to the invasion by the United States government.[2]

Interlandi's cartoon shows a woman holding a sign that reads "Get in there and save those Czech communists." She seems surprised by what she has just written and asks herself, "What am I saying?" Interlandi seems to be commenting on the outpouring of sympathy in the United States for the people of Czechoslovakia, which was surprising, given that this was the Cold War and communists and communist countries were generally considered enemies of the United States.

## 75) PETER BROOKES *Egyptian Freeze...*

Ink drawing, 24.5 × 34.5 cm. / October 17, 2000 / Published in *The Times* (London, England)

This cartoon depicts Israeli Prime Minister Ehud Barak (in office from 1999 to 2001),[1] U. S. President Bill Clinton (in office from 1993 to 2000),[2] and Yasir Arafat, who was president of the Palestinian Authority from 1996 to 2004.[3] It refers to a conference between Barak and Arafat on October 17, 2000 that was organized by Clinton and hosted by Egyptian President Hosni Mubarak. The conference was held at Sharm el-Sheikh, a resort in Egypt.

Clinton had hosted the Camp David II Summit from July 11–14 that same year. At this summit, Arafat and Barak met for peace talks, but they did not make significant progress towards ending the Israeli-Palestinian conflict.[4] A Palestinian uprising began soon after the end of the summit, prompting the parties to meet again that October in Egypt. The Israeli and Palestinian leaders did reach some agreements at this conference, but progress remained slow.[5]

In this cartoon, Brookes shows Barak, Clinton, and Arafat frozen in positions similar to those of figures in Egyptian friezes. Clinton is between Barak and Arafat, reflecting his position as a facilitator of the negotiations. Barak and Arafat are both surrounded by images of weapons, while Clinton is surrounded by images that refer to the scandal surrounding his affair with Monica Lewinsky.[6]

EGYPTIAN FREEZE...

## 76) MORTEN MORLAND *After Grant Wood's American Gothic*

Ink and ink wash drawing, 27.7 × 23.3 cm. / 2004 / Published in *The Times* (London, England)

In 2003, the United States government invaded Iraq based on the argument that it and its leader, Saddam Hussein, posed an imminent threat to the United States. In his 2002 State of the Union address, President George W. Bush had said Iraq was part of an "Axis of Evil" that also included Iran and North Korea. He also indicated that there was military intelligence suggesting Iraq had not complied with the United Nations Security Council's orders to disarm and still possessed weapons of mass destruction (WMDs). The U.N. passed a resolution on November 8, 2002 demanding that Iraq allow weapons inspectors to return, and the Iraqi government acquiesced. While the inspectors stated that no weapons of mass destruction had been found in their report of January 27, 2003, the U.S. administration argued that Iraq had not fully complied with the U.N. resolution. On March 20, 2003, the U.S. began bombing Baghdad, the capital of Iraq. The next day, U.S.-led ground forces started moving into the country.

Iraq was soon occupied by these forces and Hussein deposed. However, occupying forces did not find the weapons of mass destruction that had been one of the main justifications for the invasion. In January of 2004, Bush called for an inquiry into the failures of United States intelligence services.[1]

In this cartoon, Morland shows Bush and Condoleezza Rice, who was Bush's national security advisor from 2001 to 2005,[2] as the figures from Grant Wood's famous painting *American Gothic*. The figures in this painting are often interpreted as representations of the strong moral character and willpower of common Americans. Others believe, despite the artist's protestations to the contrary, that the image is a criticism of the rigidity and conservatism of common Americans.[3] Rice says, "It seems like intelligence wasn't your strong point after all" to Bush, who has a vacant expression on his face and a pitchfork with the letters W, M, and D stuck on its tines. This is obviously a comment on the U.S. intelligence failures surrounding the issue of weapons of mass destruction in Iraq. Additionally, it makes use of the perception among many of Bush's critics that he was unintelligent.[4]

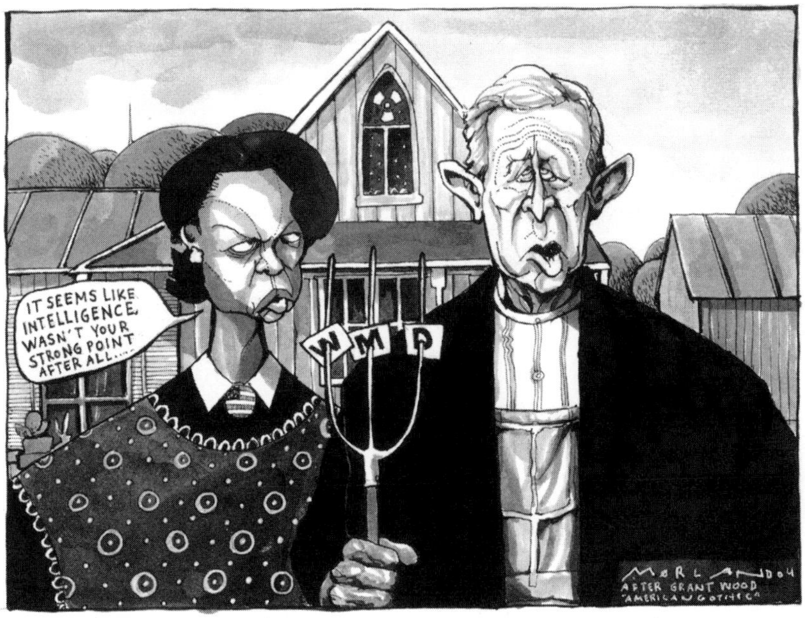
IT SEEMS LIKE INTELLIGENCE WASN'T YOUR STRONG POINT AFTER ALL...
W M D
MORLAND 04
AFTER GRANT WOOD

# NOTES

1) Fred Opper. *Another president who had a rise in the world. "From the toe-path to the White House."*

    1. "Chester Alan Arthur." *Encyclopedia of World Biography*. 2nd ed. Vol. 1. Detroit: Gale, 2004. 321–323. *Gale Virtual Reference Library*. Web. 27 May 2013, p. 322.

    2. "Roscoe Conkling." *Encyclopedia of World Biography*. 2nd ed. Vol. 4. Detroit: Gale, 2004. 201–202. *Gale Virtual Reference Library*. Web. 27 May 2013, pp. 201–202.

    3. "Chester Alan Arthur," p. 322.

    4. Doenecke, Justus, ed. "American President: A Reference Resource. American President Chester A. Arthur (1829–1886). Life Before the Presidency." *The Miller Center*. Miller Center, University of Virginia, 2013. Web. 27 May 2013. <http://millercenter.org/president/arthur/essays/biography/2>

    5. Weisberger, Bernard A. "James A. Garfield and Chester A. Arthur." *Presidents: A Reference History*. Ed. Henry F. Graff. 3rd ed. Detroit: Charles Scribner's Sons, 2002. 269–280. *Gale Virtual Reference Library*. Web. 27 May 2013, pp. 270–273.

2) Elmer A. Bushnell. *Sailing, sailing.*

    1. Kalb, Deborah, and Daniel C. Diller. "Biographies of the Vice Presidents." *The Presidents, First Ladies, and Vice Presidents: White House Biographies, 1789–2009*. Deborah Kalb, Daniel C. Diller, and Stephen L. Robertson. Washington, DC: CQ Press, 2009. 178–230. *Gale Virtual Reference Library*. Web. 18 June 2013, pp. 204–205.

    2. "Elmer A. Bushnell: Cartoonist Formerly on Globe and Journal in New York." *New York Times* 28 January 1939: 19. *ProQuest Historical Newspapers: The New York Times (1851–2009)*. Web. 18 June 2013, p. 19.

3) Lute Pease. *Their dear benefactor.*

    1. Harlow, Alvin F. "Volstead Act." *Dictionary of American History*. Ed. Stanley I. Kutler. 3rd ed. Vol. 8. New York: Charles Scribner's Sons, 2003. 352. *Gale Virtual Reference Library*. Web. 27 May 2013, p. 352.

    2. "Prohibition." *UXL Encyclopedia of U.S. History*. Sonia Benson, Daniel E. Brannen, Jr., and Rebecca Valentine. Vol. 6. Detroit: UXL, 2009. 1264–1268. *Gale Virtual Reference Library*. Web. 27 May 2013, pp. 1264–1268.

4) Art Young. *Ford for President.*

    1. "Ford, Henry." Business Leader Profiles for Students. Ed. Sheila Dow and Jaime E. Noce. Vol. 1. Detroit: Gale, 2002. 284–288. Gale Virtual Reference Library. Web. 31 May 2013, p. 284.

    2. "Ford, Henry," pp. 284–288.

    3. "Peace Ark Starts; Ford is Buoyant." New York Times 5 December 1915: 1. ProQuest Historical Newspapers: The New York Times (1851--2009). Web. 9 July 2013, p. 1.

    4. Kosek, Joseph Kip. "Henry Ford for President!" George Mason University's History News Network. George Mason University, 27 Apr. 2011. Web. 31 May 2013. <http://www.hnn.us/articles/138750.html>

    5. "The Palladium." *New York Times* 5 May 1916: 10. *ProQuest Historical Newspapers: The New York Times (1851–2009)*. Web. 31 May 2013.

    6. "Ford, Henry." *UXL Encyclopedia of World Biography*. Ed. Laura B. Tyle. Vol. 4. Detroit: UXL, 2003. 725–729. *Gale Virtual Reference Library*. Web. 31 May 2013, p. 728.

    7. "Organize for Ford, Ignoring his Wish: Backers at Detroit Conference Decide to Start a National Movement." *New York Times* 13 December 1923: 4. *ProQuest Historical Newspapers: The New York Times (1851–2009)*. Web. 31 May 2013, p. 4.

    8. "Ford for Coolidge; President Sends Him Thanks for Support." *New York Times* 20 December 1923: 1. *ProQuest Historical Newspapers: The New York Times (1851–2009)*. Web. 31 May 2013, p. 1.

    9. "Henry Ford Invents a Jewish Conspiracy." *Jewish Virtual Library*. The American-Israeli Cooperative Enterprise, 2013. Web. 18 July 2013. <http://www.jewishvirtuallibrary.org/jsource/anti-semitism/ford1.html>

    10. Boehmke, Phil. "Organizing Ford; the 1941 River Rouge strike." *American Thinker* 6 September 2010. Web. 9 July 2013.

5) Art Young. *Vice-President Marshall walks like Charlie Chaplin.*

    1. Kalb, Deborah, and Daniel C. Diller. "Biographies of the Vice Presidents." *The Presidents, First Ladies, and Vice Presidents: White House Biographies, 1789–2009.* Deborah Kalb, Daniel C. Diller, and Stephen L. Robertson. Washington, DC: CQ Press, 2009. 178–230. *Gale Virtual Reference Library.* Web. 1 June 2013, p. 206.

    2. McCaffrey, Donald W. "Chaplin, (Sir) Charles (Charlie)." *International Dictionary of Films and Filmmakers.* Ed. Sara Pendergast and Tom Pendergast. 4th ed. Vol. 3: Actors and Actresses. Detroit: St. James Press, 2000. 220–224. *Gale Virtual Reference Library.* Web. 1 June 2013, p. 223.

    3. "Folk, Joseph W. Governor of Missouri 1905–1909." *Missouri History Museum Cross Collection Search.* Missouri History Museum, 2009. Web. 1 June 2013.
        <http://collections.mohistory.org/photo/PHO:37065>

    4. "Joseph W. Folk." *St. Louis Post-Dispatch* 1 July 2010. Web. 1 June 2013.
        <http://www.stltoday.com/joseph-w-folk/image_7247e1a4-854a-11df-a60f-0017a4a78c22.html>

    5. Kalb and Diller, p. 207.

    6. Kalb and Diller, p. 207.

    7. "Woodrow Wilson." *World War I Reference Library.* Ed. Sara Pendergast, Christine Slovey, and Tom Pendergast. Vol. 2: Biographies. Detroit: UXL, 2002. 169–177. *Gale Virtual Reference Library.* Web. 1 June 2013, p. 176.

6) Art Young. *The Cabinet of Doctor Cali-Coolidge.*

    1. White, M. B. "Das Kabinett des Dr. Caligari." *International Dictionary of Films and Filmmakers.* Ed. Sara Pendergast and Tom Pendergast. 4th ed. Vol. 1: Films. Detroit: St. James Press, 2000. 620–622. *Gale Virtual Reference Library.* Web. 1 June 2013, p. 622.

    2. "A Cubistic Shocker." *New York Times* 20 March 1921: X2. *ProQuest Historical Newspapers: The New York Times (1851–2009).* Web. 1 June 2013, p. X2.

    3. McCoy, Donald R. "Coolidge, Calvin." *Presidents: A Reference History.* Ed. Henry F. Graff. 3rd ed. Detroit: Charles Scribner's Sons, 2002. 401–413. *Gale Virtual Reference Library.* Web. 1 June 2013, p. 403.

    4. "The Sacco and Vanzetti Case." *American Decades.* Ed. Judith S. Baughman, et al. Vol. 3: 1920–1929. Detroit: Gale, 2001. *Gale Virtual Reference Library.* Web. 1 June 2013.

    5. "Calvin Coolidge and Nicaragua." *American Decades Primary Sources.* Ed. Cynthia Rose. Vol. 3: 1920–1929. Detroit: Gale, 2004. 104–108. *Gale Virtual Reference Library.* Web. 1 June 2013, pp. 104–108.

    6. "Art Young, Editor and Cartoonist, 77; Crusader for Better Social Conditions 50 Years Dies Here of Heart Ailment." *New York Times* 31 December 1943: 15. *ProQuest Historical Newspapers: The New York Times (1851–2009).* Web. 1 June 2013, p. 15.

    7. "John Calvin Coolidge." *Encyclopedia of World Biography.* 2nd ed. Vol. 4. Detroit: Gale, 2004. 217–219. *Gale Virtual Reference Library.* Web. 1 June 2013, p. 218.

7) John Knott. *What this country needs is more liquid assets.*

    1. "Rainey, Henry Thomas, (1860–1934)." *Biographical Directory of the United States Congress.* Library of Congress. Web. 1 June 2013.
        <http://bioguide.congress.gov/scripts/biodisplay.pl?index=R000014>

    2. Badger, Tony. "Hundred Days." *Encyclopedia of the Great Depression.* Ed. Robert S. McElvaine. Vol. 1. New York: Macmillan Reference USA, 2004. 488–491. *Gale Virtual Reference Library.* Web. 1 June 2013, p. 488.

    3. "Legal Beer is Speeded: Cullen Bill, Drafted Upon Roosevelt Message, Has Bipartisan Support." *New York Times* 15 March 1933: 1. *ProQuest Historical Newspapers: The New York Times (1851–2009).* Web. 7 June 2013, p. 1.

    4. "3.2 Per Cent Beer Passed by Senate." *New York Times* 21 March 1933: 1. *ProQuest Historical Newspapers: The New York Times (1851–2009).* Web. 7 June 2013, p. 1.

    5. "Bottling to Start Now: Regulations Are Issued for Permits and Posting of Brewery Inspectors." *New York Times* 23 March 1933: 1. *ProQuest Historical Newspapers: The New York Times (1851–2009).* Web. 7 June 2013, p. 1.

    6. "Final Action at Capital: President Proclaims the Nation's New Policy as Utah Ratifies." *New York Times* 6 December 1933: 1. *ProQuest Historical Newspapers: The New York Times (1851–2009).* Web. 7 June 2013, p. 1.

## 8) Scott Johnston. *The walrus and the carpenter.*

1. Phelan, Craig. "Green, William." *Encyclopedia of the Great Depression*. Ed. Robert S. McElvaine. Vol. 1. New York: Macmillan Reference USA, 2004. 412–413. *Gale Virtual Reference Library*. Web. 2 June 2013, p. 412.

2. Cullen, David O'Donald. "United Brotherhood of Carpenters and Joiners." *Dictionary of American History*. Ed. Stanley I. Kutler. 3rd ed. Vol. 8. New York: Charles Scribner's Sons, 2003. 262–263. *Gale Virtual Reference Library*. Web. 1 June 2013, p. 263.

3. Lichtenstein, Nelson. "American Federation of Labor–Congress of Industrial Organizations." *Dictionary of American History*. Ed. Stanley I. Kutler. 3rd ed. Vol. 1. New York: Charles Scribner's Sons, 2003. 149–154. *Gale Virtual Reference Library*. Web. 2 June 2013, p. 150.

4. Holzka, Jane. "CIO Expelled from AFL." *St. James Encyclopedia of Labor History Worldwide*. Ed. Neil Schlager. Vol. 1. Detroit: St. James Press, 2004. 164–169. *Gale Virtual Reference Library*. Web. 2 June 2013, p. 164.

5. "Lewis, John L. 1880–1969." *American Decades*. Ed. Judith S. Baughman, et al. Vol. 4: 1930–1939. Detroit: Gale, 2001. *Gale Virtual Reference Library*. Web. 1 June 2013.

6. Paulson, Linda Dailey. "Congress of Industrial Organizations." *St. James Encyclopedia of Labor History Worldwide*. Ed. Neil Schlager. Vol. 1. Detroit: St. James Press, 2004. 221–225. *Gale Virtual Reference Library*. Web. 2 June 2013, p. 211.

7. Carroll, Lewis. *Alice's Adventures in Wonderland and Through the Looking Glass*. Ed. George Stade. New York: Barnes and Noble, 2003, pp. 190–195.

## 9) Paul Plaschke. *Mouthpiece.*

1. "Wallace, Henry A. 1888–1965." *American Decades*. Ed. Judith S. Baughman, et al. Vol. 5: 1940–1949. Detroit: Gale, 2001. *Gale Virtual Reference Library*. Web. 20 June 2013.

2. "Wallace, Henry A. 1888–1965."

3. Moscow, Warren. "Communists Back Wallace in Race, Foster Announces." *New York Times* 3 August 1948: 1. *ProQuest Historical Newspapers: The New York Times (1851–2009)*. Web. 20 June 2013, p. 1.

4. Grutzner, Charles. "Wallace is Booed at Baseball Game." *New York Times* 19 September 1948: 10. *ProQuest Historical Newspapers: The New York Times (1851–2009)*. Web. 20 June 2013, p. 10.

5. Popham, John M. "Wallace Pelted With Eggs, Fists Bang His Car in South." *New York Times* 31 August 1948: 1. *ProQuest Historical Newspapers: The New York Times (1851–2009)*. Web. 20 June 2013, p. 1.

6. "Wallace, Henry A. 1888–1965."

7. "Marshall Plan." *Europe Since 1914: Encyclopedia of the Age of War and Reconstruction*. Ed. John Merriman and Jay Winter. Vol. 3. Detroit: Charles Scribner's Sons, 2006. 1727–1731. Gale Virtual Reference Library. Web. 1 Aug. 2013, p. 1727.

8. Hogan, Michael J. *The Marshall Plan: America, Britain, and the Reconstruction of Western Europe, 1947–1952*. Cambridge: Cambridge University Press, 1987, p. 94.

9. "NATO." *Europe Since 1914: Encyclopedia of the Age of War and Reconstruction*. Ed. John Merriman and Jay Winter. Vol. 4. Detroit: Charles Scribner's Sons, 2006. 1830–1836. Gale Virtual Reference Library. Web. 1 Aug. 2013, p. 1830.

10. Hastedt, Glenn. "North Atlantic Treaty Organization (NATO)." *Encyclopedia of American Foreign Policy*. New York: Facts On File, Inc., 2004. *American History Online*. Facts On File, Inc. Web. 1 August 2013 <http://www.fofweb.com/History/MainPrintPage.asp?iPin=EAFP299&DataType=AmericanHistory&WinType=Free>

## 10) David Low. *Peaceful war news.*

1. "Stalin, Joseph." *World War II Reference Library*. Ed. Barbara C. Bigelow, et al. Vol. 3: Biographies. Detroit: UXL, 1999. 245–255. *Gale Virtual Reference Library*. Web. 21 June 2013, p. 245.

2. Marples, David R. "Malenkov, Georgy Maximilyanovich." *Encyclopedia of Russian History*. Ed. James R. Millar. Vol. 3. New York: Macmillan Reference USA, 2004. 888–890. *Gale Virtual Reference Library*. Web. 21 June 2013, p. 888.

3. "Border Violated, Czechs Say; U.S. Airmen Ridicule Charge." *New York Times* 12 March 1953: 1, 7. *ProQuest Historical Newspapers: The New York Times (1851–2009)*. Web. 21 June 2013, p. 1.

4. "Soviet MIG's Down R.A.F. Plane, Kill 5 in Berlin Air Lane." *New York Times* 13 March 1953: 1, 6. *ProQuest Historical Newspapers: The New York Times (1851–2009)*. Web. 21 June 2013, p. 1.

5. "Khrushchev, Nikita." *Cold War Reference Library*. Ed. Richard C. Hanes, Sharon M. Hanes, and Lawrence W. Baker. Vol. 4: Biographies Volume 2. Detroit: UXL, 2004. 230–240. *Gale Virtual Reference Library*. Web. 21 June 2013, p. 233.

6. Marples, p. 899.

7. "Khrushchev, Nikita," p. 233.

8. Salisbury, Harrison E. "Four to Help Rule: Beria, Molotov, Bulganin and Kaganovich Are Deputy Premiers." *New York Times* 7 March 1953: 1. *ProQuest Historical Newspapers: The New York Times (1851–2009)*. Web. 21 June 2013, p. 1.

9. "Beria, Lavrenty (1899–1953)." *Europe Since 1914: Encyclopedia of the Age of War and Reconstruction*. Ed. John Merriman and Jay Winter. Vol. 1. Detroit: Charles Scribner's Sons, 2006. 341–342. *Gale Virtual Reference Library*. Web. 21 June 2013, p. 342.

10. "Khrushchev, Nikita," p. 234.

11. Markwick, Roger D. "Mikoyan, Anastas Ivanovich." Encyclopedia of Russian History. Ed. James R. Millar. Vol. 3. New York: Macmillan Reference USA, 2004. 925. Gale Virtual Reference Library. Web. 8 July 2013, p. 925.

## 11) Joe Parrish. *Me and my shadow.*

1. Alfonso, Barry. "Humphrey, Hubert Horatio, Jr." *Scribner Encyclopedia of American Lives, Thematic Series: The 1960s*. Ed. William L. O'Neill and Kenneth T. Jackson. Vol. 1. New York: Charles Scribner's Sons, 2003. 467–469. *Gale Virtual Reference Library*. Web. 22 June 2013, pp. 468–469.

2. Solberg, Carl. *Hubert Humphrey: A Biography*. St. Paul, Minnesota: Minnesota Historical Society Press: 1984, p. 407.

3. "Muskie, Edmund Sixtus." *The Scribner Encyclopedia of American Lives*. Ed. Kenneth T. Jackson, Karen Markoe, and Arnold Markoe. Vol. 4: 1994–1996. New York: Charles Scribner's Sons, 2001. 374–376. *Gale Virtual Reference Library*. Web. 22 June 2013, p. 375.

4. Alfonso, p. 469.

## 12) Chris Riddell. *Monica under spotlights.*

1. Carl, Rollyson. "Articles of Impeachment of William Jefferson Clinton 1998." *Milestone Documents in American History: Exploring the Primary Sources That Shaped America*. Ed. Paul Finkelman and Bruce A. Lesh. Vol. 4: 1956–2003. Dallas, TX: Schlager Group, 2008. 2014–2024. Milestone Documents. Gale Virtual Reference Library. Web. 3 Aug. 2013, pp. 2014–2017.

2. Greenberg, David. "Impeachment Trial of Bill Clinton." *Dictionary of American History*. Ed. Stanley I. Kutler. 3rd ed. Vol. 4. New York: Charles Scribner's Sons, 2003. 238–241. *Gale Virtual Reference Library*. Web. 22 June 2013, pp. 238–241.

3. Simpson, Philip L. "Lewinsky, Monica (1973—)." *St. James Encyclopedia of Popular Culture*. Ed. Sara Pendergast and Tom Pendergast. Vol. 3. Detroit: St. James Press, 2000. 149–150. *Gale Virtual Reference Library*. Web. 22 June 2013, pp. 149–150.

4. Cannon, Angie, David Hess, and Robert A. Rankin. "Whitewater Prosecutor Is Replaced. The Court Chose Kenneth W. Starr. The Stunning Move Will Probably Delay The Conclusion Until 1995." *The Inquirer* 6 August 1994. *Philly.com*. Philadelphia Media Network. Web. 15 August 2013.
   <http://articles.philly.com/1994-08-06/news/25841675_1_whitewater-prosecutor-whitewater-investigation-robert-b-fiske>

5. "Text of Reno's Petition for Starr." *WashingtonPost.com*. Washington Post, 29 January 1998. Web. 15 August 2013.
   <http://www.washingtonpost.com/wp-srv/politics/special/clinton/stories/text012998.htm>

6. Brown, Derek. "1963: The Profumo Scandal." *The Guardian* 10 April 2001. Web. 11 July 2013.
   <http://www.guardian.co.uk/politics/2001/apr/10/past.derekbrown>

## 13) Paul Thomas. *P. G. Wodehouse was a traitor.*

1. Routledge, Chris. "Wodehouse, P. G. (1881–1975)." *St. James Encyclopedia of Popular Culture*. Ed. Sara Pendergast and Tom Pendergast. Vol. 5. Detroit: St. James Press, 2000. 166. *Gale Virtual Reference Library*. Web. 13 July 2013, p. 166.

2. "Wodehouse, P. G." *Gale Contextual Encyclopedia of World Literature*. Vol. 4. Detroit: Gale, 2009. 1697–1701. *Gale Virtual Reference Library*. Web. 13 July 2013, p. 1699.

3. "P. G. Wodehouse Might Have Faced Treason Charges, Files Show." *New York Times* 18 September 1999: A5. *ProQuest Historical Newspapers: The New York Times (1851–2009)*. Web. 13 July 2013, p. A5.

14) Ingram Pinn. *Lipstick war.*

1. Duclos, Susan. "Conflicting Reports About Sarah Palin's Teleprompter Problems." *Digital Journal* 4 September 2008. Web. 13 July 2013.
   <http://digitaljournal.com/article/259416>
2. "Palin's Speech at the Republican National Convention." *New York Times* 23 May 2012. Web. 13 July 2013.
3. Zeleny, Jeff. "Feeling a Challenge, Obama Sharpens His Silver Tongue." *New York Times* 10 September 2008: A20. *ProQuest Historical Newspapers: The New York Times (1851–2009)*. Web. 13 July 2013, p. A20.

15) Adalbert J. Volck ("V. Blada"). *Writing the Emancipation Proclamation.*

1. "Finding Aid to the Adalbert J. Volck Manuscript Collection, 1878–1948, MS 867." *Maryland Historical Society*. Maryland Historical Society, 2011. Web. 6 August 2013.
   <http://www.mdhs.org/findingaid/adalbert-j-volck-manuscript-collection-1878-1948-ms-867>
2. "Emancipation Proclamation." *UXL Encyclopedia of U.S. History*. Sonia Benson, Daniel E. Brannen, Jr., and Rebecca Valentine. Vol. 3. Detroit: UXL, 2009. 496–499. *Gale Virtual Reference Library*. Web. 14 July 2013, p. 496.
3. Stephenson, Wendell H. "Border War." *Dictionary of American History*. Ed. Stanley I. Kutler. 3rd ed. Vol. 1. New York: Charles Scribner's Sons, 2003. 506. *Gale Virtual Reference Library*. Web. 15 July 2013, p. 506.

16) Adalbert J. Volck ("V. Blada"). *Passage through Baltimore.*

1. Stashower, Daniel. "The Unsuccessful Plot to Kill Abraham Lincoln." *Smithsonian Magazine*. February 2013. Web. 14 July 2013.
2. Stashower, Daniel. *The Hour of Peril: The Secret Plot to Murder Lincoln Before the Civil War*. New York: St. Martin's Press, 2013, p. 266.

17) Art Young. *Stealing thunder.*

1. "The Progressive Era (1890–1930)." *Gale Encyclopedia of U.S. History: Government and Politics*. Vol. 2. Detroit: Gale, 2008. *Gale Virtual Reference Library*. Web. 15 July 2013.

18) Art Young. [Untitled] *Cartoon of two-faced Woodrow Wilson.*

1. "Wilson, Woodrow." UXL Encyclopedia of U.S. History. Sonia Benson, Daniel E. Brannen, Jr., and Rebecca Valentine. Vol. 8. Detroit: UXL, 2009. 1696–1699. *Gale Virtual Reference Library*. Web. 15 July 2013, p. 1699.
2. "Sedition Act, 1918." *American Decades Primary Sources*. Ed. Cynthia Rose. Vol. 2: 1910–1919. Detroit: Gale, 2004. 410–413. *Gale Virtual Reference Library*. Web. 15 July 2013, p. 410.
3. Krenn, Michael L. "Dominican Republic, Relations with." *Dictionary of American History*. Ed. Stanley I. Kutler. 3rd ed. Vol. 3. New York: Charles Scribner's Sons, 2003. 75–77. Gale Virtual Reference Library. Web. 15 July 2013, p. 76.
4. Santiago-Irizarry, Vilma. "Puerto Rico." *Dictionary of American History*. Ed. Stanley I. Kutler. 3rd ed. Vol. 6. New York: Charles Scribner's Sons, 2003. 543–547. Gale Virtual Reference Library. Web. 15 July 2013, p. 544–545.

19) Art Young. *The sacred bench.*

1. "William Howard Taft." *Encyclopedia of World Biography*. 2nd ed. Vol. 15. Detroit: Gale, 2004. 78–81. *Gale Virtual Reference Library*. Web. 16 July 2013, pp. 79–81.
2. "Say Taft Gets Pension from Carnegie Fund." *The Evening News* 17 April 1923: 3. Web. 15 July 2013, p. 3.
3. "Debs Attacks Taft." *The New York Times* 14 May 1923: 17. *ProQuest Historical Newspapers: The New York Times (1851–2009)*. Web. 15 July 2013, p. 17.
4. "Socialists Assail Taft." *The New York Times* 30 April 1923: 44. *ProQuest Historical Newspapers: The New York Times (1851–-2009)*. Web. 15 July 2013, p. 44.
5. "TR & Taft Split." *eHistory*. Ohio State University, 2013. Web. 3 August 2013.
   <http://ehistory.osu.edu/osu/mmh/1912/trusts/trtaft.cfm>

## 20) Daniel Dennis. *To the rescue!*

1. "The Museum Exhibit Galleries. Gallery Two: The Humanitarian Years." *Herbert Hoover Presidential Library and Museum.* Herbert Hoover Presidential Library and Museum, National Archives and Records Administration. Web. 16 July 2013. <http://hoover.archives.gov/exhibits/Hooverstory/gallery02/index.html>
2. Claussen, Martin P. "Lever Act." *Dictionary of American History.* Ed. Stanley I. Kutler. 3rd ed. Vol. 5. New York: Charles Scribner's Sons, 2003. 84. *Gale Virtual Reference Library.* Web. 16 July 2013, p. 84.
3. "Rush to Complete Embargo Details." *The New York Times* 21 June 1917: 1. *ProQuest Historical Newspapers: The New York Times (1851–2009).* Web. 15 July 2013, p. 1.
4. Claussen, p. 84.
5. "Rush to Complete Embargo Details," p. 1.
6. "The Museum Exhibit Galleries. Gallery Two: The Humanitarian Years."

## 21) Art Young. *Hoodooed.*

1. "The Museum Exhibit Galleries. Gallery Seven: From Hero to Scapegoat." *Herbert Hoover Presidential Library and Museum.* Herbert Hoover Presidential Library and Museum, National Archives and Records Administration. Web. 16 July 2013.
    <http://hoover.archives.gov/exhibits/Hooverstory/gallery07/index.html>
2. "The Museum Exhibit Galleries. Gallery Two: The Humanitarian Years." *Herbert Hoover Presidential Library and Museum.* Herbert Hoover Presidential Library and Museum, National Archives and Records Administration. Web. 16 July 2013.

## 22) Fred O. Seibel. *"Another tough one to handle."*

1. Badger, Tony. "Hundred Days." *Encyclopedia of the Great Depression.* Ed. Robert S. McElvaine. Vol. 1. New York: Macmillan Reference USA, 2004. 488–491. *Gale Virtual Reference Library.* Web. 1 June 2013, p. 488.
2. Wicker, Elmus. "Banking Panics (1930–1933)." *Encyclopedia of the Great Depression.* Ed. Robert S. McElvaine. Vol. 1. New York: Macmillan Reference USA, 2004. 88–93. Gale Virtual Reference Library. Web. 16 July 2013, p. 93.
3. "Text of the Administration Farm Relief Bill Submitted to Congress." *New York Times* 17 March 1933: 2. *ProQuest Historical Newspapers: The New York Times (1851–2009).* Web. 16 July 2013, p. 2.
4. "Government Farm Policy (Issue)." *Gale Encyclopedia of U.S. Economic History.* Ed. Thomas Carson and Mary Bonk. Vol. 1. Detroit: Gale, 1999. 388–390. Gale Virtual Reference Library. Web. 16 July 2013, p. 388.
5. Morgan, Iwan. "Economy Act of 1933." *Encyclopedia of the Great Depression.* Ed. Robert S. McElvaine. Vol. 1. New York: Macmillan Reference USA, 2004. 268–269. Gale Virtual Reference Library. Web. 16 July 2013, p. 268.
6. "Bottling to Start Now: Regulations Are Issued for Permits and Posting of Brewery Inspectors." *New York Times* 23 March 1933: 1. *ProQuest Historical Newspapers: The New York Times (1851–2009).* Web. 7 June 2013, p. 1.
7. "Legal Beer is Speeded: Cullen Bill, Drafted Upon Roosevelt Message, Has Bipartisan Support." *New York Times* 15 March 1933: 1. *ProQuest Historical Newspapers: The New York Times (1851–2009).* Web. 7 June 2013, p. 1.

## 23) Art Young. *"I will never desert you Mr. Micawber."*

1. "David Copperfield." *Novels for Students.* Ed. Ira Mark Milne. Vol. 25. Detroit: Gale, 2007. 83–109. Gale Virtual Reference Library. Web. 16 July 2013, p. 92.
2. "Unemployment Statistics during the Great Depression." *United States History.* Web. 26 July 2013.
    < http://www.u-s-history.com/pages/h1528.html>
3. "Working Women in the 1930s." *American Decades.* Ed. Vincent Tompkins. Vol. 4. Detroit: Gale, 2001. CRSN. 17 November 2010. Web. 30 July 2013.
4. "Women in the Labor Force in 2010." *United States Department of Labor.* U.S. Department of Labor, 2010. Web. 30 July 2013. <http://www.dol.gov/wb/factsheets/Qf-laborforce-10.htm>

## 24) Leslie Illingworth. *Two hearts that beat as one.*

1. Birchall, Frederick T. "Duty is Stressed at Nazi Congress." *New York Times* 8 September 1937: 10. *ProQuest Historical Newspapers: The New York Times (1851–2009).* Web. 16 July 2013, p. 10.

2. "David Copperfield." *Novels for Students*. Ed. Ira Mark Milne. Vol. 25. Detroit: Gale, 2007. 83–109. Gale Virtual Reference Library. Web. 16 July 2013, p. 92.

25) Jim Ivey. *Dominoes.*

1. "Johnson, Lyndon B." *Vietnam War Reference Library*. Vol. 1: Biographies Volume 1. Detroit: UXL, 2001. 148–164. *Gale Virtual Reference Library*. Web. 16 July 2013.

2. "The American Antiwar Movement." *Vietnam War Reference Library*. Vol. 3: Almanac. Detroit: UXL, 2001. 133–155. *Gale Virtual Reference Library*. Web. 16 July 2013, p. 138.

3. Moïse, Edwin E. "The Domino Theory." *Encyclopedia of American Foreign Policy*. Ed. Richard Dean Burns, Alexander DeConde, and Fredrik Logevall. 2nd ed. Vol. 1. New York: Charles Scribner's Sons, 2002. 551–559. *Gale Virtual Reference Library*. Web. 16 July 2013, p. 551.

4. "Kennedy, John F." *Vietnam War Reference Library*. Vol. 1: Biographies Volume 1. Detroit: UXL, 2001. 165–173. *Gale Virtual Reference Library*. Web. 16 July 2013, p. 171–172.

5. "Early American Involvement in Vietnam (1954–62)." *Vietnam War Reference Library*. Vol. 3: Almanac. Detroit: UXL, 2001. 37–59. *Gale Virtual Reference Library*. Web. 17 July 2013, p. 49–50.

26) Gib Crockett. *"Hey!--Looks like somebody's been this way before!"*

1. "Reagan, Ronald Wilson." *The Scribner Encyclopedia of American Lives*. Ed. Arnold Markoe, Karen Markoe, and Kenneth T. Jackson. Vol. 7: 2003–2005. Detroit: Charles Scribner's Sons, 2007. 446–452. *Gale Virtual Reference Library*. Web. 17 July 2013, p. 446.

2. "Reagan, Ronald Wilson," p. 448.

3. "Goldwater, Barry Morris." *The Scribner Encyclopedia of American Lives*. Ed. Kenneth T. Jackson, Karen Markoe, and Arnold Markoe. Vol. 5: 1997–1999. New York: Charles Scribner's Sons, 2002. 232–235. *Gale Virtual Reference Library*. Web. 17 July 2013, p. 234.

4. "Reagan, Ronald Wilson," p. 448–449.

5. Castro, Janice. "Press: Washington Loses a Newspaper." *Time Magazine* 3 August 1981. Web. 17 July 2013.

27) Pat Oliphant. *"Naturally, he doesn't mind what I say—I'm the ventriloquist!"*

1. Moye, J. Todd. "Andrew Young (b. 1932)." *The New Georgia Encyclopedia*. Georgia Humanities Council in partnership with the University of Georgia Press, the University System of Georgia/GALILEO, and the Office of the Governor, 1 March 2011. Web. 17 July 2013.
   <http://www.georgiaencyclopedia.org/nge/Article.jsp?id=h-1395>

2. Smith, Hedrick. "Carter's Diplomacy in Public Causing Questions and Complications." *New York Times* 15 March 1977: 6. *ProQuest Historical Newspapers: The New York Times (1851–2009)*. Web. 16 July 2013, p. 6.

28) Rick Brookes. *"John Major wants to remind you not to forget about the handshake when we catch them."*

1. Roberts, Margaret. "Oklahoma City Bombing." *Dictionary of American History*. Ed. Stanley I. Kutler. 3rd ed. Vol. 6. New York: Charles Scribner's Sons, 2003. 187–188. *Gale Virtual Reference Library*. Web. 17 July 2013, p. 187–188.

2. Pogatchnik, Shawn. "A Secret History of the IRA." *CBS News*. CBS Interactive, 11 February 2009. Web. 26 July 2013.
   <http://www.cbsnews.com/2100-511_162-524083.html>

3. "Adams, Gerry (b. 1948)." *Europe Since 1914: Encyclopedia of the Age of War and Reconstruction*. Ed. John Merriman and Jay Winter. Vol. 1. Detroit: Charles Scribner's Sons, 2006. 7–8. *Gale Virtual Reference Library*. Web. 17 July 2013, pp. 7–8.

4. "Clinton: His Role in Northern Ireland." *BBC News*. BBC, 11 December 2000. Web. 17 July 2013.
   <http://news.bbc.co.uk/2/hi/uk_news/northern_ireland/1065913.stm>

5. Greenhouse, Steven. "Gerry Adams Shakes Hands with Clinton." *New York Times*. The New York Times Company, 17 March 1995. Web. 17 July 2013.
   <http://www.nytimes.com/1995/03/17/world/gerry-adams-shakes-hands-with-clinton.html>

29) Peter Schrank. *How to Cut.*

1. "Biographies. Peter Schrank." *British Cartoon Archive*. University of Kent. Web. 17 July 2013.
   <http://www.cartoons.ac.uk/artists/peterschrank/biography>

2. Pogatchnik, Shawn. "Ireland: No deal with opposition on budget cuts." *Seattle Times.* The Seattle Times Company, 20 October 2010. Web. 17 July 2013.

&lt;http://seattletimes.com/html/businesstechnology/2013210341_apeuirelandfinancialcrisis.html&gt;

3. Corcoran, Jody and Daniel McConnell. "Cowen bails out as FF hit 8pc low." *Independent.* Independent, 23 January 2011. Web. 17 July 2013.

&lt;http://www.independent.ie/irish-news/cowen-bails-out-as-ff-hit-8pc-low-26616620.html&gt;

### 30) Art Young. *"You're a liar—I didn't eat no wahtermelon—deed I didn't."*

1. "Blacks and Watermelons." *Jim Crow Museum of Racist Memorabilia.* Ferris State University, May 2008. Web. 24 July 2013.

&lt;http://www.ferris.edu/jimcrow/question/may08/&gt;

2. "Theodore Roosevelt." *Encyclopedia of World Biography.* 2nd ed. Vol. 13. Detroit: Gale, 2004. 280–283. *Gale Virtual Reference Library.* Web. 24 July 2013, pp. 282–283.

3. "Standard Oil Check Used for Roosevelt." *New York Times* 5 October 1912: 1. *ProQuest Historical Newspapers: The New York Times (1851–2009).* Web. 24 July 2013, p. 1.

4. "Roosevelt Says Big Gifts Didn't Purchase Favor." *New York Times* 19 August 1912: 2. *ProQuest Historical Newspapers: The New York Times (1851–2009).* Web. 24 July 2013, p. 2.

5. "Blacks and Watermelons."

6. Young, Arthur. *Art Young, His Life and Times.* New York: Sheridan House, 1939, pp. 260–261.

### 31) C. N. Romanos. *The black dictator.*

1. "Holocaust Encyclopedia. Greece." *United States Holocaust Memorial Museum.* United States Holocaust Memorial Museum, June 2013. Web. 24 July 2013.

&lt;http://www.ushmm.org/wlc/en/article.php?ModuleId=10005353&gt;

### 32) Arthur Szyk. *"And what would you do with Hitler?"*

1. White, George, Jr. "African Americans, World War II." *Americans at War.* Ed. John P. Resch. Vol. 3: 1901–1945. Detroit: Macmillan Reference USA, 2005. 5–7. Gale Virtual Reference Library. Web. 26 July 2013, p. 5.

2. "African-American Soldiers in World War II Helped Pave Way for Integration of US Military." *Voice of America.* VOA News, 31 October 2009. Web. 26 July 2013.

&lt;http://www.voanews.com/content/a-13-2005-05-10-voa47-67929177/396374.html&gt;

3. "Political Art." *The Arthur Szyk Society.* The Arthur Szyk Society, 2013. Web. 26 July 2013.

&lt;http://www.szyk.org/political-art&gt;

4. Pilgrim, David. "The Golliwog Caricature." *Jim Crow Museum of Racist Memorabilia.* Ferris State University, 2012. Web. 24 July 2013.

&lt;http://www.ferris.edu/jimcrow/golliwog/&gt;

### 33) L. M. Glackens. *At the Bohemian Club.*

1. Freeman, Jo. "The Rise of Political Woman in the Election of 1912." *Women's Political History*, 2003. Web. 26 July 2013.

&lt;http://www.uic.edu/orgs/cwluherstory/jofreeman/polhistory/1912.htm&gt;

2. "Reforming Their World: Women in the Progressive Era. Introduction to Clubwomen." *The National Women's History Museum.* The National Women's History Museum, 2007. Web. 27 July 2013.

&lt;http://www.nwhm.org/online-exhibits/progressiveera/introclubwomen.html&gt;

3. Cocks, Catherine; Peter C. Holloran; and Alan Lessoff. "Feminism." *Historical Dictionary of the Progressive Era.* Lanham, Maryland: Scarecrow Press, 2009.

4. Hayes, Kevin J. "Bohemians and Vagabondia." *American History Through Literature 1870–1920.* Ed. Tom Quirk and Gary Scharnhorst. Vol. 1. Detroit: Charles Scribner's Sons, 2006. 171–176. *Gale Virtual Reference Library.* Web. 27 July 2013, p. 173.

5. "National Association Opposed to Woman Suffrage." *Encyclopaedia Britannica.* Encyclopaedia Britannica, 2013. Web. 27 July 2013.

&lt;http://www.britannica.com/EBchecked/topic/404481/National-Association-Opposed-to-Woman-Suffrage-NAOWS&gt;

6. "The Women's Suffrage Movement." *American Social Reform Movements Reference Library*. Ed. Carol Brennan, et al. Vol. 2: Almanac. Detroit: UXL, 2007. 407–441. *Gale Virtual Reference Library*. Web. 27 July 2013, pp. 429–431.

7. Smedshammer, Michael. "Clubs and Salons." *American History Through Literature 1870–1920*. Ed. Tom Quirk and Gary Scharnhorst. Vol. 1. Detroit: Charles Scribner's Sons, 2006. 267–273. *Gale Virtual Reference Library*. Web. 27 July 2013, p. 267.

### 34) Linley E. Sambourne. *Turkey and Russia.*

1. Adalian, Rouben Paul. "Hamidian (Armenian) Massacres." *Armenian National Institute*. Armenian National Institute, 2013. Web. 29 July 2013.
   <http://www.armenian-genocide.org/hamidian.html>

2. "Were ordered by the Sultan." *New York Times* 18 August 1896: 5. *ProQuest Historical Newspapers: The New York Times (1851–2009)*. Web. 29 July 2013, p. 5.

3. "Abdülhamid II." *Encyclopaedia Britannica*. Encyclopaedia Britannica, 2013. Web. 29 July 2013.
   <http://www.britannica.com/EBchecked/topic/931/Abdulhamid-II>

4. "Crete and the Powers." *New York Times* 8 June 1896: 9. *ProQuest Historical Newspapers: The New York Times (1851–2009)*. Web. 29 July 2013, p. 9.

5. Nelson, Henry Loomis. "Public Opinion: Will the Czar Change His Policy?" *New York Times* 20 September 1896: SM13. *ProQuest Historical Newspapers: The New York Times (1851–2009)*. Web. 29 July 2013, p. SM13.

6. "Turkey Backed by Russia." *New York Times* 30 November 1896: 1. *ProQuest Historical Newspapers: The New York Times (1851–2009)*. Web. 29 July 2013, p. 1.

7. "The Russian Chancellor." *New York Times* 5 September 1896: 4. *ProQuest Historical Newspapers: The New York Times (1851–2009)*. Web. 29 July 2013, p. 4.

### 35) C. N. Romanos. [Untitled] *Cartoon of Roosevelt and Jewish figures.*

1. "Rome Press Turns Fire on Roosevelt." *New York Times* 7 July 1939: 5. *ProQuest Historical Newspapers: The New York Times (1851–2009)*. Web. 30 July 2013, p. 5.

2. "Germany Ridicules President's Stand." *New York Times* 6 July 1939: 8. *ProQuest Historical Newspapers: The New York Times (1851–2009)*. Web. 30 July 2013, p. 8.

3. "Roosevelt Urges Senate to Reverse the Arms Embargo." *New York Times* 5 July 1939: 1. *ProQuest Historical Newspapers: The New York Times (1851–2009)*. Web. 30 July 2013.

4. "Roosevelt Hails Zionist Progress." *New York Times* 25 June 1939: 1. *ProQuest Historical Newspapers: The New York Times (1851–2009)*. Web. 30 July 2013.

5. "Holocaust Encyclopedia. Greece." *United States Holocaust Memorial Museum*. United States Holocaust Memorial Museum, June 2013. Web. 24 July 2013.
   <http://www.ushmm.org/wlc/en/article.php?ModuleId=10005353>

### 36) H. Strickland Constable. [Untitled] *Profiles of Aboriginal Irish Celt, Sir Isaac Newtown, and Negro.*

1. Wohl, Anthony S. "Racism and Anti-Irish Prejudice in Victorian England." *Victorian Web*. Victorian Web, 1990. Web. 30 July 2013.
   <http://www.victorianweb.org/history/race/Racism.html>

2. Coates, Ta-Nehisi. "Especially the Blacks and the Irish." *The Atlantic*. The Atlantic Monthly Group, 2 June 2010. Web. 29 July 2013.
   <http://www.theatlantic.com/personal/archive/2010/06/especially-the-blacks-and-the-irish/57556/>

### 37) Thomas Nast. *The ignorant vote—honors are easy.*

1. "Hayes, Rutherford B." *Reconstruction Era Reference Library*. Ed. Lawrence W. Baker, et al. Vol. 2: Biographies. Detroit: UXL, 2005. 113–123. *Gale Virtual Reference Library*. Web. 30 July 2013, pp. 117–118.

2. "Tilden, Samuel J." *Reconstruction Era Reference Library*. Ed. Lawrence W. Baker, et al. Vol. 2: Biographies. Detroit: UXL, 2005. 199–208. *Gale Virtual Reference Library*. Web. 30 July 2013, p. 207.

3. "Hayes, Rutherford B.," p. 119.

4. "Blacks and Watermelons." *Jim Crow Museum of Racist Memorabilia*. Ferris State University, May 2008. Web. 24 July 2013.
   <http://www.ferris.edu/jimcrow/question/may08/>

5. Wohl, Anthony S. "Racism and Anti-Irish Prejudice in Victorian England." *Victorian Web*. Victorian Web, 1990. Web. 30 July 2013.
   <http://www.victorianweb.org/history/race/Racism.html>

6. Bornstein, George. *Material Modernism: The Politics of the Page*. Cambridge: Cambridge University Press, 2001, p. 146.

7. Fitzgerald, Michael W. "Fifteenth Amendment." *Encyclopedia of African-American Culture and History*. Ed. Colin A. Palmer. 2nd ed. Vol. 2. Detroit: Macmillan Reference USA, 2006. 768–770. *Gale Virtual Reference Library*. Web. 30 July 2013, p. 769.

8. Bornstein, p. 146.

## 38) Bernhard Gillam. *Democracy's Dilemma.*

1. "American President: A Reference Resource. Key Events in the Presidency of Chester A. Arthur." *The Miller Center*. Miller Center, University of Virginia, 2013. Web. 31 July 2013.
   <http://millercenter.org/academic/americanpresident/keyevents/arthur>

2. Taussig, F. W. *The Tariff History of the United States, Part I*. New York: G. P. Putnam's Sons, Knickerbocker Press, 1910, pp. 153–154.

3. "American President: A Reference Resource. Key Events in the Presidency of Chester A. Arthur."

4. "Tariff of 1883." United States History. Web. 31 July 2013.
   <http://www.u-s-history.com/pages/h733.html>

5. "American President: A Reference Resource. Key Events in the Presidency of Chester A. Arthur."

6. Wohl, Anthony S. "Racism and Anti-Irish Prejudice in Victorian England." *Victorian Web*. Victorian Web, 1990. Web. 30 July 2013.
   <http://www.victorianweb.org/history/race/Racism.html>

7. Dunphy, Shay. "'Solid Men' – The Irish in New York Politics, 1880–1920." *The Irish Story*, 27 February 2013. Web. 31 July 2013.
   <http://www.theirishstory.com/2013/02/27/solid-men-the-irish-in-new-york-politics-1880-1920>

## 39) Kobayashi Kiyochika. *A thick-skinned face.*

1. Lehner, Monika. "Sino-Japanese War, 1894–1895." *World History Encyclopedia*. Ed. Alfred J. Andrea and Carolyn Neel. Vol. 16: Era 7: The Age of Revolutions, 1750–1914. Santa Barbara, CA: ABC-CLIO, 2011. 830–831. *Gale Virtual Reference Library*. Web. 27 May 2013, p. 830.

2. Dower, John W. "Prints and Propaganda." *Throwing Off Asia II: Woodblock Prints of the Sino-Japanese War (1894–1895)*. *Visualizing Cultures*. Massachusetts Institute of Technology, 2008. Web. 2013 June 6.
   <http://ocw.mit.edu/ans7870/21f/21f.027/throwing_off_asia_02/toa_essay01.html>

3. "Japanese art. Modern period. Wood-block prints." *Encyclopædia Britannica*. *Encyclopædia Britannica Online Library Edition*. Encyclopædia Britannica, Inc., 2013. Web. 27 May 2013.
   <http://0-library.eb.com.library.naperville-lib.org/eb/article-283317>.

4. Dudden, Alexis. *Japan's Colonization of Korea: Discourse and Power*. Honolulu, HI: University of Hawaii Press, 2006, p. 152.

5. Dower, John W. "Kiyochika's War." *Throwing Off Asia II: Woodblock Prints of the Sino-Japanese War (1894–1895)*. Visualizing Cultures. Massachusetts Institute of Technology, 2008. Web. 2013 June 6.
   <http://ocw.mit.edu/ans7870/21f/21f.027/throwing_off_asia_02/toa_essay02.html>

6. Kang, Inhye. "The Japanese Cult of the West in the Meiji Period." *World History Encyclopedia*. Ed. Alfred J. Andrea and Carolyn Neel. Vol. 14: Era 7: The Age of Revolutions, 1750–1914. Santa Barbara, CA: ABC-CLIO, 2011. 307–309. *Gale Virtual Reference Library*. Web. 27 May 2013, pp. 307–309.

7. Dower, John W. "Symbolic 'China.'" *Throwing Off Asia II: Woodblock Prints of the Sino-Japanese War (1894–1895)*. Visualizing Cultures. Massachusetts Institute of Technology, 2008. Web. 2013 June 6.
   <http://ocw.mit.edu/ans7870/21f/21f.027/throwing_off_asia_02/toa_essay05.html>

40) Bernhard Gillam. *An act forbidding Chinese immigration.*

    1. "National Capital Topics: The Persecution of the Jews in Russia." *New York Times* 3 May 1882: 2. *ProQuest Historical Newspapers: The New York Times (1851–2009).* Web. 27 May 2013, p. 2.

    2. Hamm, Michael F. "Pogroms in Russia." *World History Encyclopedia.* Ed. Alfred J. Andrea and Carolyn Neel. Vol. 18: Era 8: Crisis and Achievement, 1900–1945. Santa Barbara, CA: ABC-CLIO, 2011. 580–582. *Gale Virtual Reference Library.* Web. 27 May 2013, p. 580.

    3. "Chinese Exclusion Act." *Gale Encyclopedia of U.S. Economic History.* Ed. Thomas Carson and Mary Bonk. Vol. 1. Detroit: Gale, 1999. 162–164. *Gale Virtual Reference Library.* Web. 7 June 2013, p. 163.

    4. Wagner, Randy. "Chinese Exclusion Act 1882." *Milestone Documents in American History: Exploring the Primary Sources That Shaped America.* Ed. Paul Finkelman and Bruce A. Lesh. Vol. 2: 1824–1887. Dallas, TX: Schlager Group, 2008. 990–1002. Milestone Documents. *Gale Virtual Reference Library.* Web. 27 May 2013, p. 991.

    5. "Chinese Exclusion Act," 163.

    6. "President Harrison's Plea: He Tells Why He Signed the New Chinese Exclusion Act." *New York Times* 10 May 1882: 8. *ProQuest Historical Newspapers: The New York Times (1851–2009).* Web. 7 June 2013, p. 8.

    7. "Chinese Exclusion Act," 163.

    8. "Federation Would Bar All Orientals: Adopts Resolution Calling for Repeal of 'Gentlemen's Agreement' With Japan." *New York Times* 22 June 1921: 1. *ProQuest Historical Newspapers: The New York Times (1851–2009).* Web. 7 June 2013, p. 1.

    9. "Chinese Exclusion Act," 163.

41) Howlett. *Decorating China.*

    1. Wohl, Anthony S. "Racism and Anti-Irish Prejudice in Victorian England." *Victorian Web.* Victorian Web, 1990. Web. 30 July 2013.

    <http://www.victorianweb.org/history/race/Racism.html>

42) Otho Cushing. *I am his Uncle Sam.*

    1. "China Authorizes $30,000,000 Loan: Agreement with American, British, French, and German Financiers Approved." *New York Times* 10 May 1911: 4. *ProQuest Historical Newspapers: The New York Times (1851–2009).* Web. 27 May 2013, p. 4.

    2. Doenecke, Justus D. "Dollar Diplomacy." *Dictionary of American History.* Ed. Stanley I. Kutler. 3rd ed. Vol. 3. New York: Charles Scribner's Sons, 2003. 70–71. *Gale Virtual Reference Library.* Web. 27 May 2013, p. 71.

    3. "Russia and Japan Protest to China: Want to Take Part in $50,000,000 Loan Arranged with Bankers of Other Countries." *New York Times* 30 May 1911: 3. *ProQuest Historical Newspapers: The New York Times (1851–2009).* Web. 27 May 2013, p. 3.

    4. "Japan Vexed by China Loan: Chagrin Felt at Being Ignored in International Deal." *New York Times* 14 May 1911: 13. *ProQuest Historical Newspapers: The New York Times (1851–2009).* Web. 27 May 2013, p. 13.

    5. Coleridge, Samuel Taylor. "The Rime of the Ancient Mariner. In seven parts." *Romanticism: An Anthology.* Ed. Duncan Wu. 3rd ed. Oxford: Blackwell Publishing, 2006: 694–711.

43) Hanper. *Japan getting right before the world.*

    1. Reynolds, Douglas R. "China–Japan Relations." *Encyclopedia of Modern Asia.* Ed. Karen Christensen and David Levinson. Vol. 2. New York: Charles Scribner's Sons, 2002. 5–13. *Gale Virtual Reference Library.* Web. 27 May 2013, p. 11.

46) Martyn Turner. *"I cannot tell a lie…"*

    1. Bellesiles, Michael. "Weems, Mason Locke Parson." *Encyclopedia of the American Revolution: Library of Military History.* Ed. Harold E. Selesky. Vol. 2. Detroit: Charles Scribner's Sons, 2006. 1251. Gale Virtual Reference Library. Web. 22 July 2013, p. 1251.

    2. "The Life of Washington." *Harvard University Press.* Harvard University, 2013. Web. 22 July 2013. <http://www.hup.harvard.edu/catalog.php?isbn=9780674532519>

    3. Weems, Mason Locke. *The Life of Washington.* Ed. Marcus Cunliffe. Cambridge: Harvard University Press, 1962, p. 12.

**47) Draper Hill. *"I cannot tell a lie..."***

    1. Greenberg, David. "Impeachment Trial of Bill Clinton." *Dictionary of American History*. Ed. Stanley I. Kutler. 3rd ed. Vol. 4. New York: Charles Scribner's Sons, 2003. 238–241. *Gale Virtual Reference Library*. Web. 22 June 2013, p. 239.

**48) Art Young. *1860 the rail splitter; 1912 the lion killer.***

    1. "Roosevelt, Theodore." *Gilded Age and Progressive Era Reference Library*. Ed. Lawrence W. Baker and Rebecca Valentine. Vol. 2: Biographies. Detroit: UXL, 2007. 151–171. *Gale Virtual Reference Library*. Web. 22 July 2013, pp. 168–170.

    2. "Abraham Lincoln as 'The Railsplitter.'" *Chicago History Museum*. Chicago History Museum, 2012. Web. 22 July 2013. <http://blog.chicagohistory.org/index.php/2009/11/the-railsplitter/>

**51) John T. McCutcheon. *Cartoons of the day.***

    1. "Long Coal Strike Ends in Illinois." *New York Times* 2 October 1927: 14. *ProQuest Historical Newspapers: The New York Times (1851–2009)*. Web. 10 July 2013, p. 14.

    2. "Thompson v. McCormicks." *Time Magazine* 3 November 1930. Time, 2008. Web. 18 July 2013. <http://web.archive.org/web/20080605233217/http://www.time.com/time/magazine/article/0,9171,882358,00.html>

    3. Bukowski, Douglas. *Big Bill Thompson, Chicago, and the Politics of Image*. Champaign, IL: University of Illinois Press: 1997, p. 254.

**52) Jack B. Yeats. *A Broadside.***

    1. "Sixty Years of the Cuala Press: A Collaboration of the Yeats Family and Mollie Gill." *Boston College Libraries Newsletter*. Vol. 10, no. 1. 2008. Web. 18 July 2013. <http://www.bc.edu/libraries/newsletter/2008fall/cuala/index.html>

    2. "A Broadside." *Jack Butler Yeats Drawings and Illustrations*. Falvey Memorial Library, Villanova University, 2013. Web. 7 June 2013. <http://exhibits.library.villanova.edu/jack-butler-yeats/a-broadside>

    3. "Prints and Drawings Collection List, Harry Kernoff Collection." National Library of Ireland: 2010. Web. 18 July 2013, p. 2. <http://www.nli.ie/pdfs/PDLists/HarryKernoffPD2090TX.pdf>

    4. Ross, David A. *Critical Companion to William Butler Yeats: A Literary Reference to His Life and Work*. New York: Facts on File, 2009, p. 517.

    5. Tally, Patrick F. "Parnell, Charles Stewart." *Encyclopedia of Irish History and Culture*. Ed. James S. Donnelly, Jr. Vol. 2. Detroit: Macmillan Reference USA, 2004. 518–519. *Gale Virtual Reference Library*. Web. 19 July 2013, p. 518–519.

    6. Jordan, Donald E., Jr. "Home Rule Movement and the Irish Parliamentary Party: 1870 to 1891." *Encyclopedia of Irish History and Culture*. Ed. James S. Donnelly, Jr. Vol. 1. Detroit: Macmillan Reference USA, 2004. 299–302. *Gale Virtual Reference Library*. Web. 10 July 2013, p. 299.

    7. Sanford, John. "Roy Foster: Yeats emerged as poet of Irish Revolution, despite past political beliefs." *Stanford Report* 18 April 2001. *Stanford News*. Stanford University, 2001. Web. 7 June 2013. <http://news.stanford.edu/news/2001/april18/foster-418.html>

**53) Yoshitoshi. *Fifteen Tokugawa shoguns.***

    1. "Tokugawa Shogunate." *Gale Encyclopedia of World History: Governments*. Vol. 1. Detroit: Gale, 2008. *Gale Virtual Reference Library*. Web. 11 July 2013.

    2. Clements, Jonathan. *A Brief History of the Samurai: The Way of Japan's Elite Warriors*. London: Robinson, 2010.

    3. "Tokugawa Tsunayoshi." *Encyclopedia Britannica*. Encyclopedia Britannica, 2013. Web. 20 July 2013. <http://www.britannica.com/EBchecked/topic/598387/Tokugawa-Tsunayoshi>

    4. "Tokugawa Shogunate."

    5. "Tokugawa Yoshinobu." *Encyclopedia Britannica*. Encyclopedia Britannica, 2013. Web. 20 July 2013. <http://www.britannica.com/EBchecked/topic/598391/Tokugawa-Yoshinobu>

    6. "The Meiji Restoration." *World History Encyclopedia*. Ed. Alfred J. Andrea and Carolyn Neel. Vol. 15: Era 7: The Age

of Revolutions, 1750–1914. Santa Barbara, CA: ABC-CLIO, 2011. 536–538. Gale Virtual Reference Library. Web. 20 July 2013, p. 536–538.

54) James Gillray. *End of the Irish farce of Catholic Emancipation.*

1. "James Gillray 1757–1815. Artist Biography." *Tate.* Tate. Web. 22 July 2013.
   <http://www.tate.org.uk/art/artists/james-gillray-2739>

2. Franklin, Alexandra. "John Bull in a Dream: Fear and Fantasy in the Visual Satires of 1803." *Resisting Napoleon: The British Response to the Threat of Invasion, 1797–1815.* Ed. Mark Philp. Aldershot, UK: Ashgate Publishing, 2006, p. 125.

3. Ward, Bernard Nicolas. *The Eve of Catholic Emancipation: 1803–1812.* Volume 1. London: Longmans, Green and Co., 1911, p. 38.

4. "End of the Irish Farce of Catholic Emancipation." *Collection Online, The British Museum.* The British Museum. Web. 22 July 2013.
   <http://www.britishmuseum.org/research/collection_online/collection_object_details.aspx?objectId=1644396&partId=1>

55) George Woodward (engraved by Isaac Cruikshank). *Billy's fantoccini or John Bull over curious.*

1. Mori, Jennifer. "Pitt, William the Elder and William the Younger (1708–1778; 1759–1806)." *Europe, 1450 to 1789: Encyclopedia of the Early Modern World.* Ed. Jonathan Dewald. Vol. 4. New York: Charles Scribner's Sons, 2004. 485–487. Gale Virtual Reference Library. Web. 17 July 2013, p. 486.

2. "History. Past Prime Ministers. William Pitt 'The Younger.'" *Gov.uk.* Web. 17 July 2013.
   <https://www.gov.uk/government/history/past-prime-ministers/william-pitt>

3. "Fantoccini." *Merriam-Webster.* Merriam-Webster, Inc., 2013. Web. 17 July 2013.
   <http://www.merriam-webster.com/dictionary/fantoccini>

4. "Billy's Fantoccini or John Bull over curious." *Collection Online, The British Museum.* The British Museum. Web. 17 July 2013.
   <http://www.britishmuseum.org/research/collection_online/collection_object_details.aspx?objectId=1652786&partId=1>

56) Leslie Ward ("Spy"). *Men of the day. No. 185. Mr. John Tenniel.*

1. Allingham, Philip V. "Sir John Tenniel (1820–1914), Punch Cartoonist and Illustrator of Lewis Carroll's Alice Books." *The Victorian Web,* 3 September 2004. Web. 17 July 2013.
   <http://www.victorianweb.org/art/illustration/tenniel/pva65.html>

57) Art Young. *The blow that almost killed a cartoonist.*

1. Young, Arthur. *Art Young, His Life and Times.* New York: Sheridan House, 1939, p. 300.

58) Doug Marlette. *"Pssst! Tell me it ain't Hubert!"*

1. Alfonso, Barry. "Humphrey, Hubert Horatio, Jr." *Scribner Encyclopedia of American Lives, Thematic Series: The 1960s.* Ed. William L. O'Neill and Kenneth T. Jackson. Vol. 1. New York: Charles Scribner's Sons, 2003. 467–469. *Gale Virtual Reference Library.* Web. 22 June 2013, p. 468–469.

2. "Muskie, Edmund Sixtus." *The Scribner Encyclopedia of American Lives.* Ed. Kenneth T. Jackson, Karen Markoe, and Arnold Markoe. Vol. 4: 1994–1996. New York: Charles Scribner's Sons, 2001. 374–376. *Gale Virtual Reference Library.* Web. 22 June 2013, p. 375.

3. Alfonso, p. 469.

4. Alfonso, p. 469.

5. "McGovern, George 1922–." *American Decades.* Ed. Judith S. Baughman, et al. Vol. 8: 1970–1979. Detroit: Gale, 2001. *Gale Virtual Reference Library.* Web. 17 July 2013.

59) Unknown artist. *1960, 1964, 1968, 1972.*

1. Gustainis, J. Justin. "Counterculture." *Dictionary of American History.* Ed. Stanley I. Kutler. 3rd ed. Vol. 2. New York: Charles Scribner's Sons, 2003. 433. *Gale Virtual Reference Library.* Web. 17 July 2013, p. 433.

60) Ralph Yardley. *Autumn gusts.*

    1. "Dewey Defeats Truman." *American Decades Primary Sources*. Ed. Cynthia Rose. Vol. 5: 1940–1949. Detroit: Gale, 2004. 242–243. *Gale Virtual Reference Library*. Web. 17 July 2013, p. 242.

61) Thomas Nast. *Chancellor Bismarck "Coming to America."*

    1. "Nast, Thomas." *Gilded Age and Progressive Era Reference Library*. Ed. Lawrence W. Baker and Rebecca Valentine. Vol. 2: Biographies. Detroit: UXL, 2007. 141–149. Gale Virtual Reference Library. Web. 23 July 2013, p. 141.

    2. "Thomas Nast." *Billy Ireland Cartoon Library and Museum*. Billy Ireland Cartoon Library and Museum, Ohio State University. Web. 2 July 2013.
       <http://cartoons.osu.edu/nast/bio.htm>

    3. Lerman, Katharine Anne. "Bismarck, Otto von." *Europe 1789–1914: Encyclopedia of the Age of Industry and Empire*. Ed. John Merriman and Jay Winter. Vol. 1. Detroit: Charles Scribner's Sons, 2006. 233–242. *Gale Virtual Reference Library*. Web. 23 July 2013, p. 233.

    4. "Resignation of Prince Bismarck." *New York Times* 7 April 1880: 1. *ProQuest Historical Newspapers: The New York Times (1851–2009)*. Web. 23 July 2013, p. 1.

    5. Lerman, p. 241.

    6. Lerman, p. 237.

62) Sir John Tenniel. *Little Germanic Magnate.*

    1. Fischer, Henry W. "The Kaiser and His Family." *Munsey's Magazine* volume 12, number 1 (1894 October): 48–51.

    2. Lerman, Katharine Anne. "Bismarck, Otto von." *Europe 1789–1914: Encyclopedia of the Age of Industry and Empire*. Ed. John Merriman and Jay Winter. Vol. 1. Detroit: Charles Scribner's Sons, 2006. 233–242. *Gale Virtual Reference Library*. Web. 23 July 2013, p. 233.

    3. Lerman, p. 241.

    4. Scheck, Raffael. *Germany, 1871–1945: A Concise History*. New York: Berg, 2008, pp. 51–52.

    5. Lerman, p. 241.

    6. "The Kaiser's Conference." *New York Times* 16 March 1890: 12. *ProQuest Historical Newspapers: The New York Times (1851–2009)*. Web. 23 July 2013, p. 12.

    7. "Bismarck, Otto von (1815–1898)." *Encyclopedia of European Social History*. Ed. Peter N. Stearns. Vol. 6: Biographies/Contributors. Detroit: Charles Scribner's Sons, 2001. 21–23. *Gale Virtual Reference Library*. Web. 27 July 2013, p. 23.

    8. Cecil, Lamar. "William II." *Europe 1789–1914: Encyclopedia of the Age of Industry and Empire*. Ed. John Merriman and Jay Winter. Vol. 5. Detroit: Charles Scribner's Sons, 2006. 2468–2470. *Gale Virtual Reference Library*. Web. 23 July 2013, p. 2469.

63) E. Cusachs. *"Cab, Guv'nor?"*

    1. Garraty, John A. "Cleveland, Grover." *Presidents: A Reference History*. Ed. Henry F. Graff. 3rd ed. Detroit: Charles Scribner's Sons, 2002. 281–291. *Gale Virtual Reference Library*. Web. 31 July 2013, p. 283-286.

    2. "Stevenson, Adlai Ewing 1900–1965." *American Decades*. Ed. Judith S. Baughman, et al. Vol. 6: 1950–1959. Detroit: Gale, 2001. 218–219. *Gale Virtual Reference Library*. Web. 11 Aug. 2013, pp. 218–219.

    3. "Stevenson, Adlai Ewing III, (1930 – )." *Biographical Directory of the United States Congress*. Web. 11 August 2013.
       <http://bioguide.congress.gov/scripts/biodisplay.pl?index=s000890>

    4. Wohl, Anthony S. "Racism and Anti-Irish Prejudice in Victorian England." *Victorian Web*. Victorian Web, 1990. Web. 30 July 2013.
       <http://www.victorianweb.org/history/race/Racism.html>

    5. Dunphy, Shay. "'Solid Men' – The Irish in New York Politics, 1880–1920." *The Irish Story*. The Irish Story, 27 February 2013. Web. 31 July 2013.
       <http://www.theirishstory.com/2013/02/27/solid-men-the-irish-in-new-york-politics-1880-1920>

    6. "Our Presidents. Grover Cleveland." *The White House*. The White House. Web. 31 July 2012.
       <http://www.whitehouse.gov/about/presidents/grovercleveland22>

64) W. Carson. *They don't see me!*

1. "The Teapot Dome Scandal." *American Decades*. Ed. Judith S. Baughman, et al. Vol. 3: 1920–1929. Detroit: Gale, 2001. Gale Virtual Reference Library. Web. 31 July 2013.
2. Bennett, Leslie E. "One Lesson From History: Appointment of Special Counsel and the Investigation of the Teapot Dome Scandal." The Brookings Institution, Brooklyn College, The City University of New York, 1999. Web. 31 July 2013. <http://academic.brooklyn.cuny.edu/history/johnson/teapotdome.htm>
3. "The Teapot Dome Scandal."
4. "Prohibition." *UXL Encyclopedia of U.S. History*. Sonia Benson, Daniel E. Brannen, Jr., and Rebecca Valentine. Vol. 6. Detroit: UXL, 2009. 1264–1268. *Gale Virtual Reference Library*. Web. 27 May 2013, pp. 1264–1268.

65) Thomas Nast. *20 years a civil service reformer for himself.*

1. "Cleveland, Grover." *Gilded Age and Progressive Era Reference Library*. Ed. Lawrence W. Baker and Rebecca Valentine. Vol. 2: Biographies. Detroit: UXL, 2007. 11–24. *Gale Virtual Reference Library*. Web. 1 Aug. 2013, pp. 12–13.
2. "Nomination of James G. Blaine." *New York Times* 16 June 1876: 2. *ProQuest Historical Newspapers: The New York Times (1851–2009)*. Web. 1 August 2013, p. 2.
3. "Cartoon of the Day. The Plumed Knight." *Harpweek*. Harpweek, 2008. Web. 1 August 2013. <http://www.harpweek.com/09cartoon/BrowseByDateCartoon.asp?Month=June&Date=5>
4. Crapol, Edward P. *James G. Blaine: Architect of Empire*. Wilmington, DE: Scholarly Resources, 2000, p. 13.

66) Thomas Nast. *No upright judge would "uphold the hands of justice" like this!*

1. "Clan-na-Gael and the Murder of Dr. Cronin." *Murder by Gaslight*, 26 June 2010. Web. 1 August 2013. <http://www.murderbygaslight.com/2010/06/clan-na-gael-and-murder-of-dr-cronin.html>
2. Duke, Thomas S. "The Celebrated Murder of Dr. Cronin in Chicago." *Celebrated Criminal Cases of America*. San Francisco: J. H. Barry, 1910, pp. 406–418.
3. Kenna, Shane. "'One skilled scientist is worth an army' – The Fenian Dynamite campaign 1881–85." *The Irish Story*, 13 February 2012. Web. 6 August 2013. <http://www.theirishstory.com/2012/02/13/one-skilled-scientist-is-worth-an-army-the-fenian-dynamite-campaign-1881-85>
4. "Clan-na-Gael and the Murder of Dr. Cronin."
5. Duke, pp. 406–418.
6. "Second Edition: Six Men Indicted." *Chicago Daily Tribune* 13 October 1889: 1. *ProQuest Historical Newspapers: Chicago Tribune (1849–1989)*. Web. 1 August 2013, p. 1.

67) Arthur Young. *"Go gettem!"*

1. "Hoover, Herbert." *Great Depression and the New Deal Reference Library*. Ed. Allison McNeill, Richard C. Hanes, and Sharon M. Hanes. Vol. 2: Biographies. Detroit: UXL, 2003. 104–112. Gale Virtual Reference Library. Web. 2 Aug. 2013, p. 106.
2. Lichtman, Allan J. "Smith, Alfred E." *Encyclopedia of the Great Depression*. Ed. Robert S. McElvaine. Vol. 2. New York: Macmillan Reference USA, 2004. 890–892. Gale Virtual Reference Library. Web. 2 Aug. 2013, p. 891.
3. "Art Young, Editor and Cartoonist, 77; Crusader for Better Social Conditions 50 Years Dies Here of Heart Ailment." *New York Times* 31 December 1943: 15. *ProQuest Historical Newspapers: The New York Times (1851–2009)*. Web. 1 June 2013, p. 15.

68) Kenneth Mahood. *The Phoenix.*

1. "Prague Spring." *Europe Since 1914: Encyclopedia of the Age of War and Reconstruction*. Ed. John Merriman and Jay Winter. Vol. 4. Detroit: Charles Scribner's Sons, 2006. 2078–2082. Gale Virtual Reference Library. Web. 17 July 2013, pp. 2078–2081.
2. O'Connor, Coilin. "Jan Palach – the student whose self-immolation still haunts Czechs today." *Radio Praha*. eský rozhlas, 21 January 2009. Web. 17 July 2013. <http://www.radio.cz/en/section/czechs/jan-palach-the-student-whose-self-immolation-still-haunts-czechs-today>

3. "Velvet Revolution." *Europe Since 1914: Encyclopedia of the Age of War and Reconstruction*. Ed. John Merriman and Jay Winter. Vol. 5. Detroit: Charles Scribner's Sons, 2006. 2623–2626. *Gale Virtual Reference Library*. Web. 17 July 2013, p. 2623.

## 69) Kenneth Mahood. *Miss Czech Freedom.*

1. "Brezhnev, Leonid." Cold War Reference Library. Ed. Richard C. Hanes, Sharon M. Hanes, and Lawrence W. Baker. Vol. 3: Biographies Volume 1. Detroit: UXL, 2004. 41–52. Gale Virtual Reference Library. Web. 2 Aug. 2013, p. 41.

## 70) Arthur Young. *The man who opposes the sale of dope.*

1. "Hearst, William Randolph 1863–1951." *American Decades*. Ed. Judith S. Baughman, et al. Vol. 1: 1900–1909. Detroit: Gale, 2001. *Gale Virtual Reference Library*. Web. 2 Aug. 2013.
2. Gronert, Theodore G., and Lisa M. Tetrault. "Yellow Journalism." *Dictionary of American History*. Ed. Stanley I. Kutler. 3rd ed. Vol. 8. New York: Charles Scribner's Sons, 2003. 577. *Gale Virtual Reference Library*. Web. 2 Aug. 2013, p. 577.
3. Russell, Adrienne. "Hearst, William Randolph (1863–1951)." *St. James Encyclopedia of Popular Culture*. Ed. Sara Pendergast and Tom Pendergast. Vol. 2. Detroit: St. James Press, 2000. 379–380. Gale Virtual Reference Library. Web. 2 Aug. 2013, p. 380.
4. Russell, p. 380.

## 71) Sir Bernard Partridge. *The counter plan.*

1. "World War II." *Europe Since 1914: Encyclopedia of the Age of War and Reconstruction*. Ed. John Merriman and Jay Winter. Vol. 5. Detroit: Charles Scribner's Sons, 2006. 2766–2781. *Gale Virtual Reference Library*. Web. 3 Aug. 2013, pp. 2766–2781.
2. hakespeare, William. *Macbeth. The Complete Works of Shakespeare*. 5th ed. Ed. David Bevington. New York: Pearson, 2004, p. 1268.

## 72) Herbert Block ("Herblock"). *London.*

1. "Targeting Civilian Populations in World War II." *World History Encyclopedia*. Ed. Alfred J. Andrea and Carolyn Neel. Vol. 18: Era 8: Crisis and Achievement, 1900–1945. Santa Barbara, CA: ABC-CLIO, 2011. 603–605. Gale Virtual Reference Library. Web. 3 Aug. 2013, p. 604.
2. "London Blitz: September 1940." *American Decades Primary Sources*. Ed. Cynthia Rose. Vol. 5: 1940–1949. Detroit: Gale, 2004. 352–355. Gale Virtual Reference Library. Web. 3 Aug. 2013, p. 352.

## 73) John Chase. *Buck Truman rides again.*

1. "Dewey Defeats Truman." *American Decades Primary Sources*. Ed. Cynthia Rose. Vol. 5: 1940–1949. Detroit: Gale, 2004. 242–243. *Gale Virtual Reference Library*. Web. 17 July 2013, p. 242.
2. "Truman, Harry S." *Cold War Reference Library*. Ed. Richard C. Hanes, Sharon M. Hanes, and Lawrence W. Baker. Vol. 4: Biographies Volume 2. Detroit: UXL, 2004. 452–462. *Gale Virtual Reference Library*. Web. 3 Aug. 2013, p. 459.
3. "National Politics: Democratic Primaries and Convention 1948." *American Decades*. Ed. Judith S. Baughman, et al. Vol. 5: 1940–1949. Detroit: Gale, 2001. *Gale Virtual Reference Library*. Web. 3 Aug. 2013.
4. "Truman, Harry S.," p. 459.
5. "Wall Street Reaction." *New York Times* 4 November 1948: 28. *ProQuest Historical Newspapers: The New York Times (1851–2009)*. Web. 3 August 2013, p. 28.
6. "Truman, Harry S.," p. 459.

## 74) Frank Interlandi. *"What am I saying?"*

1. "Prague Spring." *Europe Since 1914: Encyclopedia of the Age of War and Reconstruction*. Ed. John Merriman and Jay Winter. Vol. 4. Detroit: Charles Scribner's Sons, 2006. 2078–2082. Gale Virtual Reference Library. Web. 17 July 2013, p. 2078–2082.
2. Roth, David C. *The American Reaction to the 1968 Warsaw Pact Invasion of Czechoslovakia*. Senior Honors Thesis. Ohio State University. June 2010. Web. 3 August 2013, p. 38–41.
   <http://kb.osu.edu/dspace/bitstream/handle/1811/45699/david_roth_thesis.pdf?sequence=1>

75) Peter Brookes. *Egyptian Freeze...*

1. "Barak, Ehud (1942–)." *Dictionary of the Israeli-Palestinian Conflict.* Vol. 1. Detroit: Macmillan Reference USA, 2005. 60–62. Gale Virtual Reference Library. Web. 3 Aug. 2013, p. 60.

2. "Clinton, Bill 1946-." *American Decades.* Ed. Judith S. Baughman, et al. Vol. 10: 1990–1999. Detroit: Gale, 2001. Gale Virtual Reference Library. Web. 3 Aug. 2013.

3. "Arafat, Yasir (1929–2004)." *Dictionary of the Israeli-Palestinian Conflict.* Vol. 1. Detroit: Macmillan Reference USA, 2005. 42–45. Gale Virtual Reference Library. Web. 3 Aug. 2013, p. 42.

4. "Camp David II Summit." *Dictionary of the Israeli-Palestinian Conflict.* Vol. 1. Detroit: Macmillan Reference USA, 2005. 87–88. Gale Virtual Reference Library. Web. 3 Aug. 2013, p. 87.

5. "Sixteen Years of Israeli-Palestinian Summits: Sharm el-Sheikh Conference." *Time.* Time, 17 October 2000. Web. 3 August 2013.
   <http://www.time.com/time/specials/2007/article/0,28804,1644149_1644147_1644137,00.html>

6. Simpson, Philip L. "Lewinsky, Monica (1973–)." *St. James Encyclopedia of Popular Culture.* Ed. Sara Pendergast and Tom Pendergast. Vol. 3. Detroit: St. James Press, 2000. 149–150. *Gale Virtual Reference Library.* Web. 22 June 2013, p. 149–150.

76) Morten Morland. *After Grant Wood's American Gothic.*

1. Fischbach, Michael R. "War in Iraq (2003)." *Encyclopedia of the Modern Middle East and North Africa.* Ed. Philip Mattar. 2nd ed. Vol. 4. New York: Macmillan Reference USA, 2004. 2323–2327. *Gale Virtual Reference Library.* Web. 3 Aug. 2013, pp. 2323–2327.

2. Tomassini, Christine. "Rice, Condoleezza." *Encyclopedia of African-American Culture and History.* Ed. Colin A. Palmer. 2nd ed. Vol. 5. Detroit: Macmillan Reference USA, 2006. 1947–1948. *Gale Virtual Reference Library.* Web. 3 Aug. 2013, p. 1948.

3. Price, Victoria. "American Gothic." *St. James Encyclopedia of Popular Culture.* Ed. Thomas Riggs. 2nd ed. Vol. 1. Detroit: St. James Press, 2013. 80. *Gale Virtual Reference Library.* Web. 3 Aug. 2013, p. 80.

4. Humphries, Stephen. "George W. Bush and Pop Culture's Perception." *Christian Science Monitor.* Christian Science Monitor, 23 October 2008. Web. 3 August 2013.
   <http://www.csmonitor.com/USA/Politics/2008/1023/george-w-bush-and-pop-cultures-perception>

# Index
Index of artists, publications, and select subjects. Numbers refer to catalogue entry numbers.

SET IN BULMER TYPES. PRINTED ON COUGAR OPAQUE PAPER. DESIGNED BY JERRY KELLY.